Discover the Hidden Gems of Slovakia: A Comprehensive Travel Guide

Bruna S. T. Smith

Published by ML Travel Guides, 2024.

While every precaution has been taken in the preparation of this book, the publisher assumes no responsibility for errors or omissions, or for damages resulting from the use of the information contained herein.

DISCOVER THE HIDDEN GEMS OF SLOVAKIA: A COMPREHENSIVE TRAVEL GUIDE

First edition. October 13, 2024.

ISBN: 979-8227066220

Written by Bruna S. T. Smith.

Table of Contents

Chapter 1: Introduction to the Destination

S lovakia, a hidden gem in the heart of Europe, is a nation that stands out for its natural beauty, rich history, and fascinating culture. This country, which stretches between the Alps and the Carpathian Mountains, is characterized by varied landscapes ranging from towering mountains to rolling hills and dense forests. Slovakia is a land of contrasts, where modernity blends harmoniously with centuries-old traditions, creating a unique atmosphere that attracts travelers from all over the world.

The capital, Bratislava, overlooks the Danube River and represents a meeting point between different cultures and lifestyles. Its cobbled streets, historic cafes, and bustling markets offer an insight into Slovak life. The city is dominated by Bratislava Castle, a majestic structure that stands on a hill and offers panoramic views of the river and the city below. Just a short walk from the castle, the old town is a maze of picturesque alleys, where every corner tells a story. Here, the mix of medieval, baroque and modern architecture creates a vibrant and welcoming atmosphere.

But Slovakia is not just Bratislava. Outside of the capital, the country is dotted with charming towns and villages that retain the charm of the past. Trnava, one of the oldest cities in Slovakia, is known for its historic churches and well-preserved architecture. In the Košice region, the second largest city in the country, you can admire the Cathedral of St. Elizabeth, a masterpiece of Gothic style that stands majestically in the heart of the city. Every Slovak city has its own story to tell, and visiting them is a way to discover the deep roots of this nation.

Slovakia is also a paradise for nature lovers. National parks, such as the Tatra National Park, offer stunning scenery and opportunities for outdoor activities, such as hiking, climbing, and skiing. The Tatra Mountains, with their towering peaks and crystal-clear lakes, are a great place for those seeking adventure and tranquility. Here, visitors can immerse themselves in an unspoiled environment, enjoying the beauty of the local flora and fauna.

The Slovak tradition is strongly linked to rural life and craft practices. Picturesque villages, such as Čičmany and Vlkolínec, are famous for their ornate wooden houses and traditions that are passed down from generation to generation. In these communities, artisans knit and weave, keeping ancient techniques alive and creating unique works of art. Attending a demonstration of local handicrafts is a fascinating experience that allows you to better understand Slovak culture.

Slovak gastronomy is another aspect that should not be underestimated. Traditional dishes, such as bryndzové halušky, potato dumplings with sheep's cheese, and kapustnica, a sauerkraut soup, are just some of the culinary delights that can be enjoyed. Local breweries offer a wide selection of craft beers, the result of a centuries-old tradition. Savoring typical dishes in a traditional restaurant is a way to immerse yourself in the local culture and appreciate the authentic flavors of Slovakia.

Slovakia is also a country that embraces modernity. Cities are experiencing a period of rebirth, with new architectural projects, cultural spaces and initiatives that promote contemporary art. Music festivals, art exhibitions, and cultural events enliven the Slovak calendar, offering visitors the opportunity to explore the country's art scene. This combination of tradition and innovation makes Slovakia a fascinating destination for those looking for a different and inspiring travel experience.

Another aspect that makes Slovakia unique is its strategic location in the heart of Europe. Due to its accessibility, you can easily visit neighboring countries such as Austria, Hungary, Poland, and the Czech Republic. This makes Slovakia an ideal starting point for exploring Central and Eastern Europe. Transport links are efficient, with trains and buses connecting major cities and tourist attractions.

Slovakia is also a country rich in history, with a cultural heritage that has its roots in a fascinating past. The castles, fortresses and monasteries scattered throughout the territory tell stories of knights, nobles and local traditions. Spiš Castle, one of the largest castles in Europe, is a stunning example of medieval architecture and offers a glimpse into the lives of Slovak nobles over the centuries. Equally fascinating is the Mogiła Monastery, which is an important spiritual and cultural center.

Slovakia is also a country of festivities and celebrations. Throughout the year, there are numerous events that highlight local traditions, such as fairs, markets, and folk festivals. These events provide an opportunity to interact with the locals, learn customs and traditions, and get a taste of the joy of Slovak life. Attending a traditional festival is a way to immerse yourself in the culture and to have an authentic experience.

The Slovak language, belonging to the Slavic language group, is another element that characterizes this nation. Although English is widely spoken in tourist areas, knowing a few basic phrases in Slovak can enrich the travel experience and make it easier to interact with locals. Language is a bridge that unites people and allows you to appreciate the nuances of Slovak culture.

Slovakia is a destination that invites you to explore at your leisure, allowing visitors to discover every corner and nuance of this land. From mountains to rivers, historic towns to traditional villages, each experience leaves an imprint on the heart of those who visit. The combination of nature, culture and hospitality makes Slovakia a place not to be missed, a country that deserves to be known and loved.

Embarking on a trip to Slovakia means venturing into a world rich in history and natural beauty. Each region offers something unique, from the folk traditions of rural areas to the vibrant art scenes of the cities. Slovakia is a destination that manages to surprise and enchant, always revealing new aspects and new stories to tell. It is a country that invites you to discover, to experience and to feel part of an unforgettable journey in the heart of Europe.

Chapter 2: Geographical Overview of Slovakia

S lovakia, a country nestled in the heart of Central Europe, is a place where natural beauty blends with a rich cultural history. This fascinating state, which covers an area of about 49,000 square kilometers, is characterized by a variety of landscapes ranging from majestic mountains to meandering rivers, from fertile plains to rolling hills. Its strategic position, on the border with several countries, gives Slovakia considerable geographical importance, so much so that it is a crossroads of cultures and traditions.

Located east of Austria and north of Hungary, Slovakia is bordered to the north by Poland, to the east by Ukraine, to the southwest by Austria, and to the south by Hungary. This location makes it a meeting point between different cultural and historical influences, creating a mosaic of traditions that are reflected in the daily life of its inhabitants. The country is crisscrossed by numerous rivers, including the Danube, Váh, and Hornád, which not only enrich the land but also the local culture, providing vital resources for agriculture and trade.

Slovakia is primarily mountainous, with the Carpathian Mountains dominating the northern landscape. Slovakia's Alps, particularly the Tatra, offer spectacular views and a wide range of outdoor activities, making the country a popular destination for nature lovers. These mountains are not only a paradise for hikers and skiers, but are also home to unique flora and fauna, such as roe deer, golden eagles and several species of rare plants. The Tatra mountain range stretches along the border with Poland and offers some of the highest points in Slovakia, including the Gerlachovský štít, which reaches an altitude of 2,655 meters.

Going south, the landscape turns into rolling hills and plains, where the main urban centers and agricultural areas are located. The capital, Bratislava, overlooks the Danube and represents the beating heart of the country, combining history, culture and modernity. The city, full of historical monuments, museums and vibrant nightlife, is the ideal starting point for exploring the wonders of Slovakia. Its strategic location along the Danube has not only fostered commercial development over the centuries, but has also made Bratislava a crucial hub for river transport in Europe.

Slovakia is also characterized by a continental climate, with cold winters and hot summers. This climate diversity contributes to a variety of ecosystems, ranging from coniferous forests in the northern mountains to agricultural areas in the south. National parks, such as the Tatra National Park and the Slovenský raj National Park, offer refuges for numerous species of animals and plants, making Slovakia a paradise for ecotourism lovers.

The country's natural borders are not only represented by mountains and rivers, but also by a network of nature reserves and protected areas that preserve biodiversity and natural heritage. Slovakia is a country that is actively engaging in environmental conservation, with initiatives aimed at protecting its natural resources and promoting sustainable tourism. Forests cover almost 40% of Slovakia's territory, providing vital habitats for many species and opportunities for hikers to immerse themselves in untouched nature.

Another fascinating aspect of Slovak geography is the presence of numerous caves and karst formations, such as those in the Aggtelek region and the Slovenský kras National Park. These caves, some of which are UNESCO World Heritage Sites, reveal an extraordinary underground world, with stalactites, stalagmites and underground lakes that capture the imagination of every visitor. Not only are the caves an important site of scientific research, but they are also a tourist attraction that attracts visitors from all over the world.

Slovakia is also a country rich in water resources, thanks to the presence of numerous lakes and rivers. The Danube, which flows along the southwest border, is one of the most important rivers in Europe and plays a crucial role in the country's economic and cultural life. Its waters are used for navigation, irrigation and hydroelectric power generation, contributing to the sustainable development of Slovakia. Lakes, such as Lake Štrbské Pleso and Lake Orava, offer opportunities for recreational activities, including fishing, swimming, and water sports.

Slovak cultural traditions are heavily influenced by the country's geography. The different regions, with their unique geographical characteristics, have given rise to culinary, artisanal and folkloristic traditions that reflect the diversity of the landscape. Popular festivals, often celebrated in striking natural settings, are a way for locals to honor their roots and share their culture with visitors. Events, such as the Trenčín Festival and the Bratislava Carnival, offer a unique opportunity to immerse yourself in Slovak life and discover the traditions that make this country so special.

Slovakia, with its natural wonders and central location in Europe, is a country that invites you to explore. The variety of its landscapes, the richness of its natural resources and the depth of its culture make this state a fascinating destination for travelers of all kinds. From the peaks of the Tatras to the hills of the south, from the waters of the Danube to the karst caves, Slovakia offers a unique experience that will remain in the hearts of those lucky enough to visit it. The geography of this country is not just a matter of borders and landscapes, but it is a tale of stories, traditions and natural beauty waiting to be discovered.

Chapter 3: The Historical Context of Slovakia up to 1500 AD

Slovakia, a country nestled in the heart of Central Europe, presents a fascinating mosaic of history, culture and tradition. To fully understand its identity today, it's crucial to explore its past, which unfolds through a series of key events, founding stories, and historical meanings that date back as far as 1500 AD.

The area we know today as Slovakia has been inhabited since the Stone Age, as evidenced by archaeological finds. However, it is in the period of migrations, starting from the fifth century AD, that the region begins to define itself in a more significant way. The Slavs, who settled in these lands, bring with them a culture rich in traditions and practices that will shape future generations. Slavic tribes united in a series of communities, creating territorial and social ties that would influence the political structure of the region.

In the ninth century, Slovakia became part of Great Moravia, one of the first Slavic states. This kingdom, which spanned a vast area that included parts of what is now the Czech Republic, Hungary and Austria, represented a crucial moment in the formation of the Slavic identity. The importance of Great Moravia lies not only in its political power, but also in its role as a cultural and religious center. It is here that the missionaries Cyril and Methodius introduced the Glagolitic alphabet, a fundamental step in the spread of written culture among the Slavic peoples. Their work had a lasting impact, helping to lay the foundations of Slovakia's literature and Christianization.

With the fall of Great Moravia in the 10th century, Slovakia became part of the Hungarian kingdom, which spanned much of Central Europe. This period marked a further evolution of its identity, characterized by an increasing influence on Hungarian customs and traditions. Slovakia, while retaining some of its traditions, experienced a period of cultural assimilation in which Hungarian language and social practices became predominant. The local populations found themselves living under the authority of Hungarian nobles, and political structures were reorganized to reflect Hungarian rule.

In the thirteenth century, Slovakia underwent a further transformation with the arrival of German settlers, who settled in the mining areas, thus contributing to the economic development of the region. These settlers brought with them advanced agricultural and metallurgical techniques, which helped to flourish the mining industry, especially the silver industry. Mining towns, such as Banská Štiavnica and Kremnica, became vital centers for trade and industry, contributing not only to economic prosperity, but also to Slovakia's cultural growth. The wealth from the mines resulted in a flourishing architectural development, which can still be seen today in the numerous castles and Gothic churches that dot the Slovak landscape.

The medieval period, until 1500, is also characterized by social tensions and conflicts. Struggles between the Hungarian aristocratic elites and the local peasants created a complex scenario, where rebellions and insurrections were the order of the day. The peasant class, often oppressed and heavily taxed, constantly sought to assert their rights and improve their living conditions. These social tensions helped shape the collective consciousness of Slovakia, leading to the formation of a national identity that, although still embryonic, was beginning to make its way into the hearts of the population.

In the fifteenth century, Slovakia experienced a period of crisis due to the Ottoman invasion. Turkish incursions were a constant threat, and the Hungarian kingdom had to defend its lands. Slovak communities were often at the forefront of resistance, and the struggle for survival helped to unite the various tribes and ethnic groups under a common idea of defending and protecting their lands. This experience of conflict and resistance has left a deep mark on the Slovak collective memory, giving rise to legends and stories of local heroes who fought for freedom and independence.

In addition to war and resistance, the fifteenth century also saw an increase in cultural and intellectual activity. Universities, such as the one in Pécs, attracted students from all over Europe, and Slovakia began to benefit from this cultural exchange. Oral traditions mixed with the influence of Renaissance ideas from the West, leading to a flourishing of the arts and literature. Music, poetry, and the visual arts began to reflect an increasingly defined cultural identity, which detached itself from external influences to embrace its own unique voice.

Slovakia, therefore, is not only a country of natural beauty and breathtaking landscapes, but it is also a place steeped in history and meaning. Every castle, every church, and every village tells a story of struggles, achievements, and hopes that have shaped the course of a nation. Driving through the historic streets of Bratislava, exploring the ruins of medieval castles or visiting museums dedicated to Slovak history allows you to immerse yourself in a rich and complex past, where every stone has a story to tell.

Slovakia until 1500 AD is a chapter of history that speaks of a land in continuous evolution, of cultures that intertwine and identities that are formed over time. The links with the past are evident even today, with traditions that are handed down from generation to generation, creating a sense of belonging and continuity. The experiences lived and the challenges faced have given life to a resilient nation, ready to look to the future while always keeping alive the memory of its historical roots. In this context, Slovakia emerges not only as a destination to visit, but as a place to understand and appreciate, a true historical treasure in the heart of Europe.

Chapter 4: History of Slovakia from 1500 to 1900

In the heart of Central Europe, Slovakia has experienced a rich and complex history, which is revealed through its monuments, traditions and cultural heritage. From 1500 to 1900, the Slovak territory faced a series of significant historical events that shaped its identity and destiny, creating a mosaic of cultures, languages, and influences.

During the 16th century, Slovakia was part of the Kingdom of Hungary, a vast territory under the rule of the Habsburgs. The region suffered the consequences of the wars against the Ottoman Empire, which sought to expand its rule into Central Europe. The Ottoman attacks led to the devastation of many towns and villages, and the Slovak population found themselves embroiled in conflicts that would have long-term repercussions. The battles not only caused material losses, but also a change in the social organization and structure of land ownership, with a growing power of the local nobility and an impoverishment of the peasant classes.

With the beginning of the seventeenth century, the Protestant Reformation spread to the region, leading to a religious division that would affect social and cultural life. Slovak nobles, in particular, embraced Lutheranism and other Protestant denominations, while the rural population remained largely Catholic. This religious tension resulted in internal strife and growing opposition to Habsburg authority, culminating in the Rakozzi War in the early 18th century. This revolt, led by Hungarian nobles, opposed Austrian rule and the increasing centralization of power. Although the uprising was suppressed, it marked a crucial point in Slovak history, as it highlighted the desire for autonomy and representation.

As time passed, Slovakia began to emerge as a distinctive cultural entity. In the 19th century, the Slovak national movement began to gain traction, fueled by the Enlightenment and the romantic idea of nationalism. Slovak intellectuals and poets, such as Ján Kollár and Ľudovít Štúr, played a key role in awakening national consciousness by promoting the Slovak language and cultural traditions. The Slovak language, until then considered a secondary dialect, began to gain prestige and recognition, thanks to the efforts of these pioneers who wrote literary and historical works in Slovak, thus helping to strengthen national identity.

1848 was a year of uprisings across Europe, and Slovakia was no exception. National aspirations and demands for political reform spread throughout the region. Although the Slovak revolt of 1848 against Austrian rule did not lead to the desired results, it represented a crucial moment in the process of forming Slovak identity. Ideas of freedom and self-determination began to permeate society, giving rise to a growing sense of belonging to a Slovak nation.

With the entry of Slovakia into the Austro-Hungarian Empire in 1867, the political and social dynamics changed again. Slovakia, while remaining part of Hungary, benefited from a certain autonomy and investment in infrastructure. Railways were built, connecting cities and facilitating trade. However, ethnic tensions continued to rise, with the Slovak population fighting for greater rights and recognition within a system that often favored Hungarians.

The end of the nineteenth century saw Slovakia engaged in an intense cultural and political debate. Cultural associations and literary circles flourished, promoting Slovak literature and celebrating local traditions. The thriving cities of Bratislava, Nitra and Košice became centres of cultural activity, hosting events and festivals celebrating Slovak art and music. This cultural fervour not only strengthened Slovak identity, but also helped lay the foundations for future political aspirations.

The last decade of the nineteenth century brought with it a growing political awareness and a desire for unity among the Slavic peoples. Ideas of union between the different Slavic groups of Central Europe began to gain ground, stimulating the dream of an independent Slovakia within a wider Slavic context. This vision was realized in part through the creation of cultural and political associations that sought to unite the various Slavic nationalities, creating a common front against external oppression.

In the context of these aspirations, the movement for Slovak autonomy continued to grow, culminating in a period of national awakening that would have lasting effects. Slovakia, through its historical journey from 1500 to 1900, has not only experienced conflicts and challenges, but has also given rise to a rich cultural tradition and a growing national identity. This period of history represented an important transition, in which the roots of modern Slovakia began to sprout, preparing for the dramatic changes and transformations that would follow in the twentieth century. Slovakia, with its history steeped in struggles and aspirations, stands today as a country that celebrates its historical and cultural heritage, inviting visitors to explore its stories and discover its roots.

Chapter 5: The Historical Context of Slovakia (1900 - 2024)

Slovakia, nestled in the heart of Central Europe, is a country with deep historical roots and rich in significant events. Its recent history, spanning from 1900 to the present, is characterized by a succession of events that have shaped the nation's culture, identity, and destiny. From the end of the Austro-Hungarian Empire to the creation of the Slovak Republic and modern challenges, Slovakia is an example of resilience and innovation.

At the beginning of the twentieth century, Slovakia was part of the Austro-Hungarian Empire. During this time, Slovak nationalism began to take shape. National aspirations intensified, fueled by Slovak education and literature, which sought to express the cultural identity of a people under foreign domination. 1907 marks a crucial moment with the creation of the first Slovak school in the Slovak language, a fundamental step towards the affirmation of the Slovak language and culture.

With the advent of the First World War, national tensions sharpened. Many Slovaks joined the Austro-Hungarian army, while others supported the cause for independence. The war ended in 1918 with the dissolution of the Austro-Hungarian Empire and the birth of Czechoslovakia, a new state that united Czechs and Slovaks. This union, although celebrated by many, also led to internal tensions, as the Czech majority dominated the government and institutions, often leaving the needs of the Slovaks in the background.

In the 1920s and 1930s, Slovakia sought to assert its identity within Czechoslovakia. The figure of Milan Rastislav Štefánik, a Slovak aviator and politician, became a symbol of this desire for autonomy. His tragic death in 1919 shook the country and led it to a profound reflection on its national identity. The 1930s were also marked by growing political instability in Europe, with the rise of totalitarian regimes and the threat of Nazi expansionism.

The situation culminated in 1939, when Czechoslovakia disintegrated and Slovakia declared its independence, supported by Nazi Germany. This period of autonomy was short and marked by a fascist government, with devastating consequences for the Jewish population and ethnic minorities. World War II brought destruction and suffering, but also growing resistance among Slovaks, culminating in the Slovak National Uprising of 1944, an attempt to break free from the fascist regime and Nazi occupation.

The war ended in 1945 with the victory of the Allied powers and Slovakia became part of the new socialist Czechoslovakia. Under the influence of the Soviet Union, the country underwent profound economic and social transformations. The 1950s were characterized by rapid industrialization and collectivization of agriculture, but also by repression and violations of human rights. The consequences of the communist regime were felt in all aspects of daily life, creating a climate of fear and mistrust.

In the 1960s, a reform movement, known as the "Prague Spring," sought to loosen Soviet control and promote greater political and cultural freedom. Although the movement was crushed by the invasion of Warsaw Pact troops in 1968, it left an indelible mark on the Slovak consciousness. The repression of the 1970s and 1980s led to growing discontent and the formation of dissident movements, such as the Charter 77 movement, which demanded respect for human rights.

1989 represented a crucial turning point with the fall of communism throughout Europe. Slovakia, along with the Czech Republic, actively participated in the Velvet Revolution, a peaceful movement that led to the end of the communist regime and the establishment of a democratic government. This period of transition was marked by economic and social challenges, but also by a renewed sense of national identity and hope.

In 1993, Slovakia and the Czech Republic separated peacefully, creating two independent states. The creation of the Slovak Republic was a moment of great historical significance, but also a challenge. The initial economic difficulties were accompanied by a period of political instability. However, Slovakia committed itself to building a stable democracy and a market economy, seeking to integrate further into Europe.

Slovakia's entry into the European Union in 2004 and the Schengen area in 2007 marked a new chapter in its history. These developments have opened up new opportunities for economic growth, trade and tourism. Slovakia also adopted the euro in 2009, further consolidating its position in contemporary Europe.

In the years since, Slovakia has faced several challenges, including the migrant crisis and growing disinformation. However, the country has shown remarkable resilience, continuing to promote human rights and democracy. Slovak society has seen an increase in civic participation, with an increasing number of young people actively engaging in politics and social issues.

In 2020, Slovakia faced the COVID-19 pandemic, an event that tested institutions and social cohesion. The responses of the government and civil society showed strong solidarity and a commitment to public health. The management of the health crisis has led to debates on issues of social justice and the importance of science and emergency preparedness.

In 2024, Slovakia presents itself as a dynamic country, with a vibrant civil society and a growing economy. Its recent history has forged a unique identity, characterized by a strong sense of belonging and the willingness to face future challenges. Slovakia is not only a land of natural and cultural beauty, but also a place of stories of resistance and hope, which continues to write its own chapter in the great book of European history. Visiting it means immersing yourself in a rich and complex context, where every corner, every city and every monument tells a part of this extraordinary narrative.

Chapter 6: Overview of the Local Language and Useful Phrases

When traveling to Slovakia, one of the most fascinating aspects of the local culture is undoubtedly the Slovak language. This language belonging to the Slavic branch of the Indo-European languages is spoken by over five million people, mainly in Slovakia, but also in Slovak communities abroad. The Slovak language is characterized by a rich history and a grammatical structure that can be fascinating and, at times, challenging for those who are not used to them. The language features a variety of sounds and pronunciation that can seem complex, but with a little practice, travelers can communicate effectively and immerse themselves in the local culture.

The first step in understanding the Slovak language is to familiarize yourself with the alphabet, which is based on the Latin system. The Slovak alphabet includes a few special letters, such as č, ď, ľ, ň, š, and ž, each of which has a specific sound. For example, the letter "š" is pronounced as "sh" in English, while "č" is pronounced as "ch". Interestingly, the Slovak language is phonetic, which means that words are pronounced as they are written, which helps a lot in learning.

For travelers venturing into Slovakia, knowing a few useful phrases can greatly facilitate everyday interactions. One of the most common phrases you can use is "Dobrý deň", which means "Good morning". This greeting is appropriate in almost all daytime situations and is generally greeted with a smile. When meeting up with someone in a more casual setting, you can opt for "Ahoj," which is equivalent to "Hello." Interestingly, the friendliness of the Slovak greeting can open doors and create a friendly atmosphere.

Another key expression is "Ďakujem", which means "Thank you". In Slovakia, gratitude is highly valued, and saying this word can help establish a good relationship with the locals. If you want to be even more courteous, you can say "Ďakujem veľmi pekne", which means "Thank you very much". Similarly, if you need to apologize, "Prepáčte" is the word to use, which translates to "Excuse me."

When exploring the country, you're likely to ask for road information or directions. In this case, "Kde je...?" is a very useful question, which means "Where is it...?". For example, "Kde je nádražie?" asks "Where is the station?" It is important to note that the locals are usually very helpful and ready to help tourists, so don't hesitate to ask for information.

Another crucial expression is "Koľko to stojí?", which means "How much does it cost?". This phrase will be especially useful in markets, shops or restaurants. When it comes to ordering food and drinks, it's helpful to know how to say "Môžem si objednať?" which means "Can I order?". In addition, "Jedlo" means "food" and "Nápoj" means "drink", terms that can facilitate communication in restaurants.

As far as numbers go, knowing the numbers in Slovak can be a big plus. The numbers from one to ten are: jeden (1), dva (2), tri (3), štyri (4), päť (5), šesť (6), sedem (7), osem (8), deväť (9), and desať (10). Familiarizing yourself with these numbers not only helps you shop, but it's also helpful in understanding public transit directions and schedules.

Another area where knowledge of the Slovak language can be helpful is in seeking help or medical information. Phrases such as "Potrebujem pomoc" which means "I need help" or "Kde je najbližšia nemocnica?" which translates as "Where is the nearest hospital?" can prove invaluable in emergency situations.

Slovak culture is deeply rooted in local traditions and celebrations, and many of these are linked to specific phrases and idioms. For example, during the holidays, it is common to hear "Šťastný nový rok" to wish "Happy New Year". Knowing these expressions can enrich the travel experience and show respect for the local culture.

In Slovakia, hospitality is a core value, and locals are often happy to share their language and culture with visitors. Attending local events or festivals offers a unique opportunity to practice the language and immerse yourself in Slovak daily life. Attend a market, sample traditional cuisine, and exchange a few words with vendors. Even simple conversations can leave a lasting impression and create meaningful connections.

When traveling, it's normal to feel a little overwhelmed by the language barrier. However, the key is to have a positive and open attitude. Even if you don't master the Slovak language, trying to speak Slovak will be appreciated by the locals. Slovaks often respond in English or other languages, but your effort to communicate in their native language will be enthusiastically received.

Another interesting aspect of the Slovak language is its influence from other languages. Due to Slovakia's geographical location and history, the language has absorbed elements from German, Hungarian, and Czech languages, among others. This enriches the Slovak vocabulary and makes it interesting to study the origins of certain words. Additionally, having similar words in Italian or other Romance languages can help travelers make connections and memorize words more easily.

Slovakia is a country rich in natural beauty, history, and culture, and language is a gateway to explore all of these. Each city, village and region has its own unique character, and knowing the language helps to perceive its essence. From the capital Bratislava, with its bustling streets and vibrant nightlife, to the picturesque villages of the Tatra Mountains, every corner of Slovakia tells a story that can best be understood through words.

A trip to Slovakia is an opportunity to not only visit a new country, but also to learn and grow through interaction with the language and culture. Every word you say, every phrase you practice, contributes to creating indelible memories. So, get ready to explore, communicate, and discover all that Slovakia has to offer, and never forget the power of language to connect people and create meaningful experiences.

Chapter 7: Population, Culture and Traditions of Slovakia

Slovakia, a charming country in the heart of Central Europe, boasts a population that reflects its complex and fascinating history. With more than five million inhabitants, Slovakia is characterized by ethnic diversity that enriches its social fabric. The majority of its citizens are ethnic Slovaks, but significant minorities are also present, including Hungarians, Roma, and Czechs. This ethnic diversity is reflected in the traditions, languages, and cultural celebrations that animate the country.

The official language is Slovak, a West Slavic language that shares similarities with Czech and Polish. Language is a crucial element of national identity and is used in all spheres of public life. However, in regions with a strong presence of minorities, such as in the south of the country, Hungarian is widely spoken, thus contributing to a rich and varied linguistic landscape. Language is a vehicle for a living culture, and local dialects add an extra layer of uniqueness to everyday communication.

Slovakia has a cultural history deeply rooted in folk traditions, which are passed down from generation to generation. Festivals and celebrations are crucial moments for the community, in which ancient rituals and modern influences are mixed. Easter, for example, is celebrated with unique rituals, such as the tradition of "šibačka", where boys hit girls with willow branches to wish them fertility and good health. These customs reflect a deep connection to nature and the cycles of life.

Music and dance are equally vital in Slovak cultural life. Folk melodies, often accompanied by traditional instruments such as the hurdy-gurdy and double bass, resonate during the celebrations. Folk dance groups, dressed in colorful and richly decorated costumes, perform at local festivals and events, telling stories of daily life and historical legends. Music is a universal language that brings people together, and in Slovakia, it is a celebration of community and cultural roots.

Religion plays a significant role in the lives of the Slovak population. The majority of the population is Catholic, with a significant presence of other denominations, such as Protestantism and Orthodoxy. Catholic churches dot the urban and rural landscape, serving not only as places of worship, but also as community centers. Religious celebrations are often accompanied by social events that involve the whole community, creating a sense of belonging and solidarity.

Sacred architecture is another fascinating aspect of Slovak culture. The Gothic and Baroque churches, with their imposing towers and artistic details, tell stories of faith and tradition. St. Martin's Cathedral in Bratislava and St. Elizabeth's Church in Košice are just two examples of how art and architecture come together to reflect the nation's spirituality. These places are not only centers of worship, but also testimonies to Slovakia's rich artistic history.

Gastronomic traditions are another fundamental aspect of Slovak identity. The hearty and varied local cuisine is based on fresh, seasonal ingredients. Dishes such as "bryndzové halušky", potato dumplings with sheep's cheese, and "kapustnica", a sauerkraut soup, are an integral part of the daily diet. Parties and celebrations are often accompanied by an abundance of food and drink, creating occasions for conviviality and merriment. Slovak wine, known for its quality, is an essential part of the celebrations, with regions such as Tokaj wine standing out for their fine production.

Handicraft traditions are another expression of Slovak culture. The art of ceramics, woodworking, and traditional embroidery are just some of the artistic forms that reflect the creativity and skill of local artisans. Craft markets, held in different towns and villages, offer visitors the opportunity to purchase unique and authentic pieces while supporting local economies.

Education is a core value in Slovakia, and the country has a well-developed education system. Universities, such as Comenius University in Bratislava, are renowned for their academic excellence and attract students from all over the world. The culture of reading is widespread, and public libraries play a crucial role in promoting Slovak literature, with authors such as Milan Kunder and Dominik Tatarka helping to give the nation a voice.

Slovakia is also a country that values its recent history. The peaceful transition from Czechoslovakia to independence in 1993 is a pivotal moment that marked a new era for the country. The commemoration of historical events, such as the Velvet Revolution, is an important part of the national consciousness, celebrated through festivals, exhibitions and public debates. The historical memory is preserved in museums and monuments scattered throughout the territory, which tell the struggle for freedom and national identity.

Respect for the environment and sustainability are values that are increasingly present in Slovak culture. The country's natural wonders, such as the Tatra Mountains and numerous protected areas, are a source of pride for citizens. Ecological initiatives and festivals dedicated to nature promote environmental awareness and love for natural heritage. Slovakia is a paradise for nature lovers, with hiking trails that pass through stunning landscapes and offer opportunities for exploration and adventure.

In terms of sports, football and ice hockey are the most popular disciplines, with a strong passion on the part of Slovaks. National team matches are events that bring communities together, creating a sense of belonging and pride. International competitions see Slovakia compete with determination, and Slovak athletes are often considered ambassadors for the nation, bringing Slovak culture and spirit around the world.

Slovakia is a country that thrives on contrasts, where modernity blends with tradition. Vibrant cities, such as Bratislava and Košice, offer a mix of contemporary and historical culture, with art galleries, theaters, and festivals celebrating local creativity. At the same time, picturesque villages and rural areas maintain a slower pace of life, allowing you to appreciate the beauty of everyday life and traditions.

This country, with its warm and welcoming population, invites travelers to discover not only its natural landscapes but also the richness of its cultural traditions. Every corner of Slovakia tells a story, and every encounter with local people is an opportunity to understand and appreciate their unique identity. Slovakia is a journey through time and space, where history, culture and everyday life are intertwined in a fascinating tapestry of experiences.

Chapter 8: Climate and Best Seasons to Travel in Slovakia

Slovakia, a jewel in the heart of Europe, is a country that offers a varied and fascinating climate, perfect for every type of traveler. Its geographical location, nestled between the Alps and the Pannonian plains, contributes to a climatic diversity that makes every visit a unique experience. Throughout the year, the seasons alternate with a well-defined rhythm, offering ever-changing views and atmospheres. In this chapter, we will explore the climatic characteristics of Slovakia, analyzing the different seasons and suggesting the best times to discover this enchanting country.

The Slovak climate is continental, characterized by cold winters and hot summers. Temperatures can vary greatly from one season to the next, creating a rich and varied weather landscape. In general, summers are hot, with temperatures ranging between 25 and 35 degrees Celsius, while winters can drop below freezing, especially in mountainous areas.

Spring, which runs from March to May, is a time of awakening and rebirth. With the arrival of March, temperatures begin to rise and nature awakens from winter hibernation. The days are getting longer and the sun is starting to get hotter. In March, average temperatures hover around 10 degrees Celsius, while in April and May they approach 15-20 degrees. Spring is a great time to visit Slovakian cities, where flowers begin to bloom and parks are filled with vibrant colors. Slovak traditions come alive with different festivals and markets, making this a perfect time to immerse yourself in the local culture. Spring is also a great season for hiking in the Tatra Mountains, where the trails are cleared of snow and you can take in breathtaking views.

Summer, which stretches from June to August, is undoubtedly the most popular season for tourists. The days are long and sunny, with temperatures that can exceed 30 degrees, especially in the southern regions. Cities such as Bratislava, Košice and Prešov come alive with cultural events, festivals and open-air concerts. This is an ideal time to explore historic castles and national parks, where you can enjoy outdoor activities such as hiking, cycling, and water sports. Slovakia's thermal waters, famous throughout Europe, are highly sought after during the summer, offering a perfect way to relax after a day of exploring. However, it is important to consider that July and August can also bring afternoon thunderstorms, so it is advisable to be prepared for any changes in the weather.

Autumn, which runs from September to November, is another lovely season to visit Slovakia. Temperatures are starting to drop, but the weather is still pleasant, with sunny days and cool nights. September is particularly mild, with temperatures hovering around 20 degrees, while October and November see a drop to around 10-15 degrees. The leaves of the trees begin to change color, creating an extraordinary natural spectacle, especially in mountainous areas and national parks. This is an ideal time for hiking and enjoying the beauty of Slovak nature. In addition, autumn is the grape harvest season, and many wine-growing regions offer tours and tastings, allowing you to discover fine Slovak wines.

Winter, which runs from December to February, transforms Slovakia into a fairytale country, covered in a blanket of snow. Temperatures can drop well below freezing, especially in mountainous areas, where ski resorts such as Jasná and Tatranská Lomnica become popular destinations for winter sports enthusiasts. Slovak winters are characterized by cold days and freezing nights, with temperatures ranging from -5 to 5 degrees. Cities dress up for the Christmas holidays, with markets offering handicrafts, typical sweets and hot drinks. This is a perfect time to explore Slovak traditions and savor the Christmas atmosphere.

For those looking to avoid the tourist crowds, the off-season months, such as November and March, can prove to be particularly beneficial. During these times, you can explore the beauties of Slovakia in peace, taking advantage of lower rates for hotels and tourist attractions. In addition, spring and autumn offer unique colors and atmospheres, making every visit a memorable experience.

Despite the climatic differences between the various seasons, Slovakia always has something to offer. Every time of year brings with it new opportunities to explore and discover. Whether summer hikes in the mountains, visits to Christmas markets or autumn winery tours, Slovakia is a country that invites you to discover in all its facets. With careful planning and an eye on the weather forecast, every traveler will be able to fully experience the enchantment of this country, being guided by the seasons and the beauty of the nature that surrounds it.

Ultimately, whether you choose to visit Slovakia in spring, summer, autumn, or winter, there is always a reason to appreciate this country rich in history, culture, and stunning scenery. The key to an unforgettable trip lies in understanding the climate and seasons, so you can better plan your adventures and fully immerse yourself in the Slovak experience.

Chapter 9: Transport Options in Slovakia

Slovakia, located in the heart of Central Europe, is a fascinating country that offers a variety of transportation options for every type of traveler. With its stunning landscapes, historic cities, and rich culture, exploring this country becomes an exciting and accessible adventure thanks to a well-developed transportation network. In this chapter, we will explore the main modes of transportation available, from major airports to train stations and bus routes.

The main airport in Slovakia is Bratislava Airport, located a few kilometers from the capital. This international stopover is the ideal starting point for those looking to explore the country and beyond. With connections from several European cities, the airport offers numerous low-cost and scheduled flights, making Bratislava easily accessible. Once landed, visitors can take advantage of several transportation options to reach the city center. Public buses, operated by Bratislavská Integrovaná Doprava, provide a regular and convenient service, while taxis and ride-sharing services such as Uber are readily available for those who prefer a more direct and private journey.

In addition to Bratislava Airport, there are other airports that deserve attention. Košice Airport, located in Slovakia's second largest city, offers domestic and international connections, especially to European destinations. This stopover is especially useful for those looking to visit the eastern sector of the country, which is known for its natural landscapes and unique culture. Poprad-Tatry Airport, located near the Tatra National Park, is another option for those looking to explore the Slovak mountains. With seasonal flights and an increasing number of connections, this airport is a popular choice among nature lovers and winter sports enthusiasts.

Once you land, Slovakia offers a well-organized public transportation system that includes trains and buses. The Slovak railway network, operated by Železnice Slovenskej republiky (Slovak Railways), is an excellent way to get around the country. Trains connect major cities such as Bratislava, Košice, Prešov, and Nitra, making travel between them quick and easy. Express trains, which offer modern and comfortable facilities, are particularly popular with travelers. Train stations are usually well-equipped, with information available in English and other languages, making it easy for tourists to find their way around.

Bratislava Central Station, located in the heart of the capital, is a major railway junction connecting Slovakia to several European destinations. From here, travelers can take direct trains to Vienna, Budapest, and Prague, making Bratislava an excellent starting point for exploring neighboring countries as well. Trains to Košice depart regularly, and the journey through the Slovak countryside offers spectacular views of the mountains and valleys. Travelers should take note of train schedules, as they can vary, and it is recommended to purchase tickets in advance, especially during peak tourist season.

The bus system in Slovakia is equally efficient and offers extensive connections between towns and villages. The buses are operated by several companies, including Slovak Lines and RegioJet, which offer high-quality services with modern and comfortable buses. Bus stations, such as the main one in Bratislava, are well organized and provide information on routes and schedules. Buses are an excellent option for those looking to visit locations that are less accessible, such as the picturesque villages of the Tatra Mountains or the historic castles scattered throughout the country.

Another mode of transportation that is gaining popularity is car-sharing and car rental, which is especially useful for those looking to explore remote areas or follow customized itineraries. Several car rental companies operate in Slovakia, both at airports and in major cities. Renting a car allows you to move around with greater freedom and discover hidden places that may not be easily accessible by public transport. Slovak roads are generally in good condition and well-signposted, making driving an enjoyable experience.

For those who prefer a more authentic and scenic experience, bicycles are an eco-friendly and fun option. Many Slovak cities, including Bratislava and Košice, offer bike-sharing services that allow visitors to rent bicycles to explore urban centers and surrounding areas. Slovakia is known for its well-maintained cycling routes, with routes that pass through natural and historical landscapes. Cyclists can enjoy routes along the Danube River, which offers spectacular views and the opportunity to stop at various points of interest along the way.

Finally, it is worth mentioning private transport, such as taxis and ride-sharing services, which are very common in Slovak cities. Taxis are readily available, and drivers are usually professional and helpful. However, it is advisable to use ride-sharing apps for more transparency on costs and availability. These services can be especially useful overnight or on special occasions, when you want direct and stress-free transportation.

In conclusion, Slovakia offers a comprehensive range of transportation options that meet the needs of every traveler. Whether international flights, panoramic trains, comfortable buses or renting a car, the country is easily accessible and invites you to explore. Each mode of transport offers a unique opportunity to discover the beauty and diversity of Slovakia, making each trip a memorable experience.

Chapter 10: Visa and Entry Requirements

When it comes to planning a trip to Slovakia, one of the first things to consider is the visa and entry requirements. Slovakia, an integral part of the European Union and the Schengen zone, has an entry system that varies depending on the nationality of the traveler. For Europeans, the procedures are typically simpler, while visitors from outside Europe must pay more attention to specific requirements.

For citizens of member countries of the European Union and the European Economic Area, entry into Slovakia is a relatively smooth process. No visa is required, and travelers can enter the country by simply presenting a valid ID, such as a national ID card. It is important, however, that the document is valid and that the traveler has proof of residence or a return ticket with them in case it is requested. Although it is not common, Slovak authorities may ask to see proof of travel and accommodation, especially in the case of more thorough checks.

For third-country nationals, the rules are more complex and vary greatly. The first thing to check is whether your country has a visa waiver agreement with Slovakia. For example, citizens of the United States, Canada, Australia, and some Asian nations can enter Slovakia without a short-stay visa, generally up to 90 days, as long as the trip is not motivated by work or study. Again, you must present a valid passport, which must remain in force for at least three months beyond your intended date of departure from Slovakia.

For those who do not fall into the visa waiver categories, you must apply for a Schengen visa. This type of visa allows you to travel not only to Slovakia, but also to all other member countries of the Schengen area. The application process for a Schengen visa may seem complex, but by following a few basic steps, it becomes manageable. The first thing you need to do is determine the type of visa you need. There are different types of Schengen visas, depending on the purpose of the trip: tourism, business, study, or visiting family and friends.

Once you have identified your visa type, the next step is to gather the necessary documentation. Generally, a variety of documents are required, including a completed application form, a recent passport-sized photo, a copy of your valid passport, and proof of round-trip flight booking. In addition, you must prove that you have valid health insurance for the duration of your stay, which covers any medical expenses up to a minimum of 30,000 euros.

Another crucial document is proof of accommodation, which can be a hotel reservation, a rental agreement, or a letter of invitation from a Slovak resident. If you plan to stay with friends or family, it is advisable to include a copy of the host's ID, along with the invitation letter. This help can simplify the visa approval process by proving that you have a place to stay overnight.

After gathering all the necessary documents, you should proceed to book an appointment at the Slovak embassy or consulate in your country of residence. During the appointment, you will need to submit documentation, and in some cases, a personal interview may also be required. It is important to arrive prepared and on time, as delays or missing documents can compromise the request.

The processing time for a Schengen visa can vary, but it is generally recommended that you submit your application at least three weeks before departure. In some cases, the process can take up to a month or more, so it's wise not to leave everything to the last minute. Once approved, the visa will be affixed to your passport and will be valid for a specific period, depending on the type of visa you apply for.

In addition to visa requirements, it is essential to know the Slovak customs regulations. Upon entry into the country, travelers must declare certain goods and comply with restrictions on the importation of goods. For example, there are limits on the amounts of alcohol and tobacco that can be brought into Slovakia without having to pay customs duties. Travelers can carry up to one liter of alcohol above 22 degrees, while for spirits below this strength, the amount can be up to two liters. As for tobacco, you are allowed to bring up to 200 cigarettes, 100 cigars or 50 grams of smoking tobacco.

In addition, it is forbidden to import drugs and hazardous materials. Travelers should exercise caution with food and plant products, as the import of certain foods or plants may be restricted to prevent the spread of diseases and pests. It is always advisable to inquire in advance about what is allowed and what is best to avoid bringing.

For those traveling with pets, a specific procedure must be followed. Pets must be accompanied by a pet passport, which proves vaccination against rabies and other diseases. Additionally, it is advisable to consult with your veterinarian before embarking on your trip to ensure that all requirements are met.

Finally, another important aspect to keep in mind is the health situation. In recent times, due to global events such as the COVID-19 pandemic, some health requirements may have been introduced and may vary. It is essential to find out about the current regulations regarding vaccinations, testing, and any quarantines that may be required upon entry into the country.

In conclusion, Slovakia is a fascinating and accessible destination for travelers from all over the world. However, it is crucial to pay attention to visa and entry requirements, to ensure a smooth arrival. With the right preparation and understanding of the current regulations, explorers can fully enjoy the wonders this country has to offer, from its historic medieval towns to breathtaking natural landscapes. Make sure you have all the documents in order and are informed about customs regulations for a smooth and worry-free trip.

Chapter 11: Travel Tips for Novice Visitors

Visiting Slovakia for the first time is an experience that promises to be as compelling as it is revealing. This country, rich in history, culture and breathtaking landscapes, offers travelers a unique mix of tradition and modernity. However, to fully enjoy this trip, it is essential to be prepared. In this chapter, we'll explore some essential tips for first-time visitors, focusing on practicalities such as currency exchange, travel insurance options, and other helpful tips to make your experience in Slovakia unforgettable.

When it comes to currency, Slovakia uses the euro (EUR), which greatly simplifies the financial issue for travelers coming from European countries. However, it's important to note that for people from countries outside the Eurozone, currency exchange can be a bit more complicated. Before you travel, it is advisable to find out about the current exchange rates for the euro against your local currency. Banks and bureaux de change in large cities offer competitive rates, but it's always a good idea to compare rates before making the transaction.

In case you prefer to withdraw money, you can use ATMs, which are widely available in cities and tourist centers. Credit cards are accepted in most hotels, restaurants and shops, although it is advisable to always have some cash on hand for small purchases or in more rural areas where cards may not be accepted. In addition, it is useful to inform your bank about traveling abroad to prevent transactions from being blocked for security reasons.

Another crucial aspect to consider before embarking on a trip to Slovakia is travel insurance. Although it is not mandatory, it is strongly recommended, as it can offer important protection in case of unforeseen events. A good travel insurance plan should cover medical expenses, trip cancellation, theft or loss of personal property, and assistance in case of emergencies. It is advisable to compare different policies and read the conditions carefully, in order to choose the one that best suits your needs. Some credit cards also offer travel insurance coverage, so it's worth researching these benefits before purchasing a separate policy.

Another useful tip for first-time visitors is to familiarize yourself with the local customs and regulations. Slovakia is a hospitable country, but as in any part of the world, there are certain cultural practices to be respected. For example, when entering a house or place of worship, it is customary to take off your shoes. Also, it's important to be aware of time differences: Slovakia is located in the Central European Time Zone, which is one hour ahead of Coordinated Universal Time (UTC+1).

As far as internal transport is concerned, Slovakia offers a well-developed public transport network. Trains and buses connect major cities and tourist spots, making it easy to get around without having to rent a car. Train stations are generally efficient and well-signposted, and tickets can be purchased in advance online or directly at the station. If you plan to visit multiple places, it may be helpful to consider purchasing a transportation pass that allows unlimited travel for a set amount of time.

Slovakia is also famous for its beautiful natural landscapes, from the Tatra Mountains to the many national parks. For nature lovers, it is imperative to prepare properly for hiking. Wearing comfortable shoes and carrying a bottle of water and light snacks is essential. Additionally, it's important to check the weather forecast, as conditions can change quickly, especially in the mountains.

When it comes to food and drink, Slovakia offers a variety of delicious dishes that are worth trying. Slovak cuisine is characterized by fresh ingredients and traditional recipes. Be sure to savor bryndzové halušky, potato dumplings with sheep's cheese, and kapustnica, a sauerkraut soup. Restaurants can vary greatly in price and quality, so it's helpful to ask locals for recommendations or consult online reviews before choosing where to eat.

Finally, don't forget to bring a power adapter with you, as the sockets in Slovakia are type C and F, with a voltage of 230 V and a frequency of 50 Hz. This is especially important if you want to use electronic devices such as smartphones, tablets, or laptops. Make sure you have everything you need before you leave, to avoid any inconveniences during your stay.

Slovakia is a country that offers a lot to visitors, but proper preparation is crucial to make the most of the experience. With good planning and an open mind, your trip to Slovakia is sure to be memorable. Knowing local practices, being aware of your own safety, and managing financial matters are essential steps in enjoying a smooth vacation. With these tips, you'll be ready to explore all that this fascinating country has to offer, from its historic cities to its beautiful natural landscapes.

Chapter 12: Booking Tips and Best Areas to Stay

When it comes to visiting Slovakia, one of the first decisions that every traveler faces is where to stay overnight. Your choice of accommodation can greatly influence the overall travel experience, making it essential to consider not only the type of accommodation, but also the area where you decide to stay. Slovakia, with its charming historic towns, quaint villages, and spectacular mountain ranges, offers a wide range of options to suit every type of traveler. In this chapter, we'll explore the best neighborhoods and provide helpful tips on how to book the ideal accommodation.

Let's start with Bratislava, the Slovak capital, which is a perfect starting point for exploring the country. This city is a fascinating mix of history, culture and modernity. Visitors can find a variety of accommodation options, from luxurious five-star facilities to cozy apartments for rent. The old town, known as Staré Mesto, is a great choice for those looking to immerse themselves in city life. Here, you can admire the cobbled streets, outdoor cafes, and numerous historical monuments, such as Bratislava Castle and St. Martin's Cathedral. Staying in the historic center allows you to easily explore all the main tourist attractions on foot.

Another popular area is the modern part of the city, which is home to a number of contemporary hotels and offers a vibrant nightlife. The areas around the Danube, in particular, are renowned for their trendy restaurants and bars, which are popular with locals and tourists alike. Booking a hotel with a river view can offer a unique experience, especially at sunset, when the city lights reflect off the serene waters.

For those looking for a quieter, more residential atmosphere, the Petržalka and Karlova Ves neighborhoods can be an interesting alternative. These areas, located a short distance from the center, offer an excellent opportunity to live like a local. Here, you can find apartments and long-term rentals at more affordable prices, making these areas ideal for extended stays.

In addition to Bratislava, it is worth considering other Slovak cities for your stay. Košice, the country's second-largest city, is a fascinating place with a rich history and a vibrant cultural scene. Košice's Old Town is well-preserved and offers a variety of accommodation options, from cozy guesthouses to luxury hotels. St. Elizabeth's Cathedral and Liberty Street are just a few of the attractions that can be easily explored from hotels located in the center.

Trnava, known as the "Slovak Rome" due to its number of churches, is another city worth a visit. Here, travelers can stay in charming bed and breakfasts or boutique hotels that reflect the city's historic character. Trnava is easily accessible from Bratislava, making it an ideal choice for a day trip or longer stay.

If the goal is to explore nature, the Tatra Mountains are a must-see destination. The towns of Poprad and Štrbské Pleso offer a wide range of accommodation, from mountain hotels to cosy chalets. These areas are perfect for outdoor enthusiasts, as they offer direct access to hiking trails, ski resorts, and beautiful panoramic views. Booking in advance during the ski season is recommended, as these areas can quickly fill up with tourists.

When it comes to booking accommodation, there are a few practical tips to keep in mind. First of all, it's crucial to do thorough research. Using online booking platforms allows you to compare prices and read guest reviews. Never neglect reviews, as they can provide valuable insights into other travelers' experiences. It's also helpful to check hotel websites, as they often offer more competitive rates and exclusive promotions.

Another important aspect to consider is the flexibility of your travel dates. If possible, try to avoid peak seasons, such as summer and holidays, when prices can increase significantly. Traveling during spring or fall can not only guarantee lower fares but also a more favorable climate to explore.

The location of the accommodation is crucial. Make sure to choose an area that is well-connected by public transportation, especially if you plan to visit multiple cities or attractions. In Slovakia, the public transport system is generally efficient, but having accommodation close to tram or bus stops can make getting around much more convenient.

Don't forget to consider the type of experience you want to have. If you are looking for a luxurious stay, international hotel chains and high-end resorts are available in major cities. However, if you want a more authentic atmosphere, private rentals and small guesthouses can offer more direct contact with the local culture. In addition, staying at a guesthouse can provide an opportunity to interact with the owners and receive advice on what to see and do in the surrounding area.

One aspect to take into account is free cancellation. Many hotels and apartments offer this option, which can be very useful if you have a change in your travel plans. Please make sure to read the cancellation policies carefully before confirming your booking.

For those traveling on a budget, there are several budget-friendly options available in Slovakia. Hostels are a popular choice among young travelers and offer affordable rates with the option to stay in shared or private rooms. In addition, some cities also offer well-equipped campsites, ideal for those who love to be in contact with nature.

Finally, don't forget to take advantage of the special offers during your stay. Many hotels and restaurants offer promotional packages that may include breakfast, guided tours, or discounts on local attractions. Being flexible with your dates and accommodation choices can lead to significant savings.

In summary, Slovakia offers a wide range of accommodation options to suit every need and preference. Whether it's a stay in the heart of Bratislava, in a picturesque town like Trnava or in a mountain hut in the Tatras, it's essential to do your research thoroughly and book in advance. Considering the location, amenities offered, and guest reviews can help ensure a memorable travel experience. With a little planning and preparation, your stay in Slovakia will undoubtedly be an adventure to remember.

Chapter 13: Top Landmarks and Monuments of Slovakia

Slovakia is a country rich in history, culture and natural beauty, a real treasure in the heart of Central Europe. Among its breathtaking landscapes and fascinating traditions, some of the most significant monuments and historical places that tell the story and identity of this nation stand majestic. This chapter will explore some of Slovakia's most iconic landmarks, inviting travelers to discover the stories behind them.

We start our journey with Bratislava Castle, an undisputed symbol of the Slovak capital. Located on a hill overlooking the Danube River, the castle has a history dating back to Roman times. Its origins can be traced back to the ninth century, when it served as a fortification. Today, its impressive Baroque architecture and pyramid-shaped towers attract visitors from all over the world. Inside, the castle houses the Museum of the History of Slovakia, where you can see archaeological finds and works of art that tell the story of Slovak life and culture over the centuries. Walking through the surrounding gardens, visitors can enjoy spectacular views of the city and the Danube, making this place a must-see.

Continuing our route, we arrive at Trenčín Castle, one of the most impressive medieval fortresses in Slovakia. Located on a rock overlooking the town of Trenčín, this castle has a strategic location that dates back to the thirteenth century. Legend has it that the castle was built on a Roman fortress, and its thick walls and towering towers tell stories of battles and sieges. Inside, visitors can explore the frescoed rooms, corridors, and exhibits dedicated to Slovakia's medieval history. The panoramic view from the top of the walls is undoubtedly one of the highlights of the visit, offering an enchanting view of the valley below and the surrounding mountains.

Another architectural gem is Bojnice Castle, known for its fairytale appearance. Located in the village of Bojnice, this castle was built in the twelfth century and has undergone numerous restorations over the centuries. Its Gothic architecture and romantic charm make it one of the most photographed castles in Slovakia. Inside, the castle is furnished with period furniture and artwork that tells the story of the Slovak nobility. Don't miss the chance to also visit the famous Bojnice Zoo, located nearby, which offers a unique experience for families and animal lovers.

We cannot forget the Grassalkovich Palace, the official residence of the President of Slovakia, located in Bratislava. This palace, built in the eighteenth century, is an outstanding example of Baroque architecture. Its elegant rooms are often open to the public for events and guided tours. The gardens surrounding the palace are a great place for a serene stroll, with fountains and flower beds framing the building's beauty. This place is not only a symbol of Slovak political power, but also an important cultural center that hosts events and concerts throughout the year.

Continuing our journey, we move towards the center of Spiš, where Spiš Castle is located, one of the largest castles in Europe and a UNESCO World Heritage Site. Its construction began in the eleventh century and the current structure is the result of centuries of extensions and restorations. The panoramic position of the castle, on a hill that offers a spectacular view of the surrounding region, makes this place particularly impressive. Visitors can explore the castle ruins, admiring the impressive walls and towers, while inside you can find exhibits documenting the history of the castle and the region. The beauty of the surrounding landscape, with its green fields and distant mountains, contributes to making this visit an unforgettable experience.

Not far from here is the town of Levoča, famous for its Church of St. James, another UNESCO site. This Gothic church, built in the fifteenth century, is known for its carved wooden main altar, which is considered one of the largest and most beautiful in Europe. Every detail of the altar tells religious and historical stories, attracting the attention of artists and visitors alike. Levoča's main square, with its colorful houses and lively atmosphere, is a great place to savor local cuisine and immerse yourself in Slovak culture.

Another must-see monument is the Church of St. Elizabeth in Košice, the largest cathedral in Slovakia. This Gothic church was built between the thirteenth and fourteenth centuries and is a masterpiece of medieval architecture. Its elaborate façade, stunning stained glass windows, and 60-meter-high bell tower make it one of the most visited tourist attractions in the country. Inside, visitors can admire statues, frescoes, and an atmosphere of sacredness that invites reflection. The square in front of the cathedral is often bustling with cultural events and markets, offering an authentic experience of Slovak life.

We cannot forget the Slavin National Monument, located on a hill overlooking Bratislava. This memorial is dedicated to the Soviet soldiers who lost their lives during World War II. The panoramic view from the top is breathtaking, allowing you to admire the entire city and the Danube River. The central sculpture and memorial plaques make this place an important site of remembrance and reflection, while visitors can stroll through the tree-lined avenues and enjoy a moment of tranquility.

A trip to Slovakia is not complete without a visit to Low Tatras National Park, where the famous Demänovská Cave is located. This extraordinary natural formation is known for its spectacular stalactites and stalagmites. The cave is open to the public and offers guided tours that lead visitors through fascinating galleries, telling the geological history and local legends. The surrounding area is perfect for hiking and outdoor activities, making this place a paradise for nature lovers.

Finally, we head to the picturesque town of Nitra, where the Nitra Castle is located. This castle, which dominates the city, has a history dating back over a thousand years. Today, the castle houses a museum that exhibits the history of Slovakia and its traditions. The view from the top of the castle walls is spectacular, offering a glimpse into the city and the surrounding landscapes. Nitra is also famous for its Cathedral of St. Emeric, an example of Romanesque architecture that is worth a visit.

These sites represent only a part of the wonders that Slovakia has to offer. Each monument and landmark tells a unique story, a piece of the puzzle that makes up the rich history and culture of this country. Slovakia is a land of contrasts, where the past and present intertwine, creating an unforgettable travel experience. With its castles, churches, and historical monuments, every corner of this country invites you to discover and explore, making every visit an opportunity to immerse yourself in the beauty and charm of Slovakia.

Chapter 14: Museums and Cultural Institutions in Slovakia

Slovakia, enshrined in the heart of Europe, is a country with a rich cultural and artistic history, reflected in its many museums and cultural institutions. Through the centuries, the Slovak territory has seen the influence of different civilizations, each of which has left an indelible mark on the country's cultural heritage. Slovak museums not only offer an in-depth look at local history and culture, but are also custodians of priceless works of art, testimonies to a vibrant and complex past.

The capital Bratislava is undoubtedly the hub of the country's cultural life. Here you will find the Slovak National Museum, an impressive institution that spans the history of Slovakia from its origins to the present day. With several locations scattered throughout the city, the museum is a veritable treasure trove of information, with exhibits ranging from prehistory to contemporary art. The collections of folk art, architecture, and natural history provide visitors with a varied and immersive experience. One cannot help but be fascinated by the temporary exhibitions that often highlight emerging Slovak artists, making the museum an ever-changing place.

Another place of great relevance is the Bratislava City Museum, located in the striking Grassalkovich Palace. This museum tells the story of the capital through a collection of archaeological finds, paintings, photographs, and historical documents. The building itself, with its baroque architecture, is a work of art that is worth admiring. The museum's halls also host cultural events and temporary exhibitions, making this space an important meeting point for artists and citizens.

Not far from Bratislava, in the picturesque village of Modra, is the Museum of Ceramics, dedicated to the tradition of Slovak ceramics. Modra pottery is famous for its beauty and unique design, and this museum offers a unique opportunity to discover the production process and craft techniques used over the centuries. Visitors can also participate in hands-on workshops, learning how to create their own ceramic artwork under the guidance of expert artisans.

Continuing our cultural journey, we head north, to the city of Nitra, where the Regional Museum is located. This museum illustrates the history of the Nitra region, with a focus on local culture and traditions. The exhibits include archaeological finds, art, and artifacts that date back to ancient times, making the museum a fascinating place for those looking to learn more about Slovak history. The beauty of the collections is amplified by the location of the museum, immersed in a historical and natural context of great value.

Another cultural gem is the Academy of Fine Arts and Design in Bratislava, which not only serves as an educational institution but also houses exhibition galleries that are open to the public. Works by students and emerging artists are exhibited here, creating a dynamic and stimulating environment where contemporary Slovak design can be appreciated. Exhibitions change frequently, always offering new perspectives on modern art and design trends.

The city of Košice, the second largest in Slovakia, is another cultural center of importance. The Museum of History of the City of Košice welcomes visitors with a rich collection that tells the local history through historical objects, photographs and works of art. The city is also famous for its Gothic architecture, and the museum is located near St. Elizabeth's Cathedral, making it easily accessible for a visit. Throughout the year, Košice hosts various cultural events and festivals, making the museum a hotspot for the community.

We cannot forget the Museum of Slovak Music, located in Bratislava, which celebrates the country's rich musical heritage. The collections include historical musical instruments, sheet music and documents that highlight the evolution of music in Slovakia. The museum regularly organizes concerts and events, offering visitors the chance to immerse themselves in Slovak musical culture in an engaging and interactive way.

In another corner of Bratislava is the Centre for Contemporary Art – Kunsthalle Bratislava, dedicated to Slovak and international contemporary art. This versatile space hosts temporary exhibitions, workshops and conferences, becoming a reference point for artists, students and art enthusiasts. The Kunsthalle is committed to promoting dialogue between artists and audiences, creating a stimulating environment for creativity and innovation.

The Museum of the History of Slovakia, located in Bratislava, offers insight into the country's history through a wide range of exhibits and documents. The exhibits tell the story of Slovak history from its origins to modern times, with a particular emphasis on the key events that shaped national identity. Here, visitors can explore the evolution of Slovakia through a visual narrative that makes history accessible and engaging.

Slovakia is also famous for its castles, many of which house museums that tell the story of the nobility and daily life in past centuries. Bratislava Castle, for example, is not only a symbol of the capital, but also an important museum site. Its historic rooms have been restored and furnished to reflect the lives of the nobles who inhabited the castle, offering visitors an insight into aristocratic life. The panoramic views from the top of the castle over the city and the Danube are an added incentive to visit this historic structure.

The Bratislava Automobile Museum is another must-see attraction for motor enthusiasts. This unique institution collects a wide range of historic and modern vehicles, telling the story of the Slovak automotive industry. The exhibits include rare models and prototypes, offering a comprehensive overview of the evolution of automotive design and technology in the country.

A trip to Slovakia would not be complete without visiting the many cultural centers that are dedicated to the promotion of folk traditions. One of them is the Rajecká Lesná Folk Traditions Centre, where visitors can learn about traditional Slovak customs, music and dances. Events and festivals are held here regularly, allowing visitors to enjoy live performances and actively participate in craft workshops.

Finally, we cannot overlook the importance of the contemporary art galleries that dot the Slovak territory. The Slovak National Gallery, based in Bratislava, is an institution of international significance that promotes Slovak and foreign art through prestigious exhibitions. This gallery aims to connect the public with contemporary art, offering events, conferences and workshops involving artists, critics and art lovers.

As we immerse ourselves in Slovak culture through its museums and institutions, it is evident that each visit offers a unique opportunity to explore the history, art, and traditions of a fascinating country. Slovakia, with its rich cultural offer, presents itself as a must-see destination for anyone wishing to discover the deep roots and evolution of a nation that continues to amaze and inspire.

Chapter 15: Natural Wonders and Parks of Slovakia

<hr>

Slovakia, a hidden gem in the heart of Europe, is a country of stunning natural beauty, stretching from the towering Tatra Alps to the rolling hills of the Pannonian region. This chapter will explore the natural wonders and national parks of Slovakia, inviting travelers to immerse themselves in breathtaking landscapes and discover the rich biodiversity that characterizes this nation.

We start our journey at the Tatra National Park, one of the most famous destinations in Slovakia. This protected area, which stretches along the Polish border, is famous for its jagged peaks, crystal-clear lakes, and lush forests. Mount Gerlach, the highest peak in the country, offers spectacular views and is an unmissable challenge for experienced hikers. Well-marked trails allow you to explore the beauty of the Tatras, with trails winding through pine forests and alpine grasslands.

The Tatra National Park is also a refuge for wildlife. Here you can spot animals such as brown bear, chamois and wolf. Bird lovers will find a wide range of species, including the rare golden eagle. Spring is a particularly fascinating time to visit the park, as wildflowers bloom and fill the meadows with vibrant colors.

Continuing our journey, we head to the Slovenský Raj National Park, or the Slovak Paradise, known for its deep gorges, spectacular waterfalls and impenetrable forests. This park is a true paradise for climbers and hikers, with trails climbing along rock faces and wooden bridges spanning rushing streams. The hike through the Suchá Belá Gorge is one of the most exciting experiences, with a route that includes wooden stairs and narrow passages that lead to spectacular waterfalls.

Slovenský Raj National Park is also a great place for families, who can enjoy quieter walks on the less demanding trails. During the summer, the park is a cool and shady refuge, while in autumn the leaves of the trees are tinged with golden and red shades, creating a natural spectacle of incomparable beauty.

Another natural jewel of Slovakia is the Pieniny National Park, located along the border with Poland. This park is famous for its Dunajec River, which offers exciting raft rides between steep cliffs and lush forests. Sailing on the Dunajec is a unique experience, allowing you to admire the beauty of the surrounding landscape and discover the rich history and culture of the region. Traditional rafts, built of wood and guided by local experts, offer a fascinating way to explore the park and experience an unforgettable adventure.

Pieniny National Park is also a place of great importance for biodiversity. Numerous species of plants and animals can be found here, many of which are rare or endangered. During a walk in the park, you can come across wild orchids and rare birds, making each visit a unique and valuable experience.

Slovakia's natural wonders are not limited to national parks. The country's many nature reserves provide additional opportunities to explore the beauty of the Slovak landscape. The Karpatská Nature Reserve, located in the heart of the Carpathian Alps, is a perfect example of how nature can thrive in a protected environment. This place is characterized by ancient forests, crystal-clear streams, and diverse wildlife, making it an ideal retreat for nature lovers and those looking for some tranquility away from the hustle and bustle of modern life.

In summer, nature reserves offer a cool retreat, while in winter they are transformed into enchanting landscapes covered in snow. The Karpatská Nature Reserve is also an ideal destination for birdwatching, with opportunities to spot many migratory species that stop here on their journey.

We cannot forget to mention the historic gardens of Slovakia, which offer a unique fusion of art and nature. The Bratislava Garden, located in the heart of the capital, is an example of how botanical beauty can be integrated with history. This garden features a variety of rare plants and colorful flowers, and is a great place for a relaxing walk or family picnic.

In addition, the Bratislava Botanical Garden is a true oasis of tranquility in the chaos of the city. Here, visitors can explore a wide range of plants from around the world, with paths winding through flower beds and greenhouses filled with exotic vegetation. This garden is a perfect place to learn more about Slovak and international flora, with exhibits showcasing the beauty and diversity of plants.

Another notable garden is the Vysoké Tatry Garden, located in the foothills of the Tatra Alps. This garden is dedicated to mountain flora, with a variety of alpine plants and rare species. While visiting, travelers can admire the vibrant colors of the mountain flowers and enjoy spectacular views of the surrounding mountains.

For those who want a more adventurous experience, Slovakia offers plenty of hiking routes and outdoor activities, allowing you to explore the country's stunning landscapes. The Tatra Alps, with their well-maintained trails, are ideal for day hikes or multi-day treks. Hikers can choose from a variety of routes, from the easiest and most scenic to the most challenging ones that lead to high peaks.

Water activities are equally popular, with rivers and lakes offering opportunities for rafting, kayaking, and fishing. The Váh River, the longest in Slovakia, is a popular destination for water sports, while the lakes of Štrbské Pleso and Popradské Pleso are ideal for a day of relaxation and fun.

Slovakia, with its rich variety of national parks, nature reserves and historic gardens, is a true paradise for nature lovers. Every corner of this country tells a story, a deep bond between man and nature that has stood the test of time. Visiting these places is not only an opportunity to admire the beauty of the Slovak landscape, but also an invitation to reflect on the need to protect and preserve these treasures for future generations. Slovakia is a place where nature reigns supreme, and every visit promises to leave an indelible mark on the hearts of those lucky enough to explore it.

Chapter 16: The Wonders of Bratislava

Bratislava, the capital of Slovakia, is a city that enchants with its fusion of history, culture and modernity. Located on the banks of the Danube River, it offers a fascinating panorama and a vibrant atmosphere that attracts visitors from all over the world. Walking through its cobbled streets, you can feel the echo of bygone eras, while the contemporary architecture integrates harmoniously with the historical monuments. The city is a true crossroads of cultures, where Austrian, Hungarian and Czech influences intertwine in a unique mosaic.

One of the most recognizable symbols of Bratislava is Bratislava Castle, which towers over the city like a silent guardian. With its white towers and distinctive red roof, the castle offers spectacular views of the Danube and its surroundings. Its history dates back to the prehistoric period, but the current shape was mainly shaped during the Baroque period. Within the walls, visitors can explore the Slovak National Museum, which houses an extensive collection of art and historical artifacts, providing a great insight into Slovak culture.

On the way down from the castle, you find yourself in the old town, where picturesque squares and narrow cobbled streets invite you to a leisurely stroll. The main square, Hlavné námestie, is the beating heart of the city. Here you can admire the Old Town Hall, a splendid Gothic building that dates back to the fifteenth century, with its tower offering a panoramic view of the city. In this square, cultural events and markets are regularly held, making it a lively and dynamic place.

Not far from here, you will find the Church of St. Martin, another emblematic monument of Bratislava. This church, famous for its tall tower and Gothic architecture, has witnessed important historical events, including the coronations of Hungarian kings. The interiors are decorated with frescoes and works of art, which tell stories of faith and tradition. The church is an active place of worship and an important landmark for the citizens of Bratislava.

For those who want to immerse themselves in local life, the Mercato di Pugliese is a must-see. Located in the city center, this market offers a variety of fresh produce, local crafts, and culinary specialties. Here you can savor traditional Slovak dishes, such as bryndzové halušky, potato dumplings with sheep's cheese, and enjoy a glass of Slovak wine, renowned for its quality and variety. The market is also a great place to interact with locals and learn about the region's culinary traditions.

Continuing our journey, we cannot forget the New Bridge, a modern architectural work that connects the old town with the more modern district of Petržalka. This bridge, with its distinctive pole-shaped structure, offers spectacular views of the Danube and the city. Below the bridge is the UFO restaurant, famous for its panoramic views and innovative cuisine. Climbing to the top of the bridge at sunset is an unforgettable experience, with the sky tinged with golden and red hues as the sun reflects off the waters of the river.

Bratislava is also a vibrant cultural hub, with numerous museums and art galleries. The Slovak National Gallery is a must-visit place for art lovers, housing an extensive collection of works ranging from the medieval period to contemporary art. The exhibitions include works by Slovak and international artists, offering an insight into the history of art in Slovakia and around the world.

Another interesting attraction is the Bratislava City Museum, located in an old Baroque palace. Here you can discover the origins of the city, its evolution over the centuries and the main events that have shaped it. Interactive exhibits and historical artifacts make for an engaging and informative visit, perfect for those looking to delve deeper into local history.

The Žilina district, located a few kilometers from Bratislava, is worth a visit for its historic architecture and fascinating monuments. The Church of St. John the Baptist, with its slender bell tower and ornate interior, is a perfect example of Gothic architecture. In addition, Žilina Castle, located on a hill, offers a panoramic view of the city and a charming walk through its gardens.

During the summer season, Bratislava comes alive with festivals and outdoor events. The Bratislava Music Festival attracts internationally renowned artists and offers concerts of various musical genres, from classical music to jazz. The Wine Festival is also an unmissable event for lovers of good drinking, with tastings of Slovak wines and traditional local culinary dishes. These events offer an excellent opportunity to immerse yourself in Slovak culture and discover the gastronomic traditions of the region.

For those looking for a bit of relaxation, Sad Janka Kráľa Park is an oasis of tranquility in the heart of the city. This park, one of the oldest public gardens in Europe, is a great place for walks, picnics, and moments of contemplation. Its tree-lined paths, ponds, and flower beds create a serene atmosphere, perfect for escaping the hustle and bustle of urban life.

Another must-see attraction is the Grassalkovich Palace, the official residence of the President of Slovakia. This elegant palace, surrounded by beautiful gardens, is a stunning example of Baroque architecture. Although access inside is limited, visitors can take in the beauty of the exterior and stroll through the manicured gardens.

Bratislava is also a great starting point for exploring the natural beauty of Slovakia. The nearby Tatra Mountains offer stunning views and opportunities for hiking, skiing, and outdoor activities. The historic towns of Trnava and Nitra, with their ancient churches and charming squares, are just a short drive away and are well worth a visit. These places offer an opportunity to discover Slovak history and immerse yourself in the local culture.

Bratislava's nightlife is equally interesting, with a variety of bars, clubs, and restaurants enlivening the city's evenings. From live music in traditional pubs to modern nightclubs, there's something for everyone to enjoy. The bars along the Danube offer a romantic atmosphere, perfect for enjoying a cocktail while contemplating the reflection of the lights on the surface of the water.

Bratislava, with its rich history, vibrant culture, and natural beauty, is a destination that captivates and surprises. Every corner of the city tells a story, every street invites you to explore. Ending the day with a walk along the Danube, admiring the illuminated castle and the night view, is an experience that will remain in the heart of every visitor. The city is a treasure to be discovered, a gem in the heart of Europe that deserves to be experienced and appreciated.

Chapter 17: The Wonders of Bratislava

Bratislava, the capital of Slovakia, is a city that embodies the fusion of history, culture and modernity. Among its many attractions, Bratislava Castle stands as the second most visited site in the country, attracting thousands of tourists from all over the world every year. This impressive castle, located on a hill overlooking the course of the Danube River, is not only a testament to Slovak history, but also a symbol of the country's resilience and architectural beauty.

The history of Bratislava Castle has its roots in the ninth century, when it was built as a strategic outpost against invasions. Over the centuries, the castle has undergone numerous alterations and expansions, reflecting the different architectural styles and cultural influences that have followed. From its prime location, the castle offers a breathtaking panoramic view of the city and the surrounding landscape, making it an ideal place for photography lovers and those looking to immerse themselves in the beauty of Slovak nature.

Arriving at the castle, you are greeted by a majestic door that invites you to cross the threshold of this place steeped in history. The façade, characterized by elegant lines and architectural details, features a mix of styles ranging from baroque to neoclassical. The towers that soar into the sky are adorned with cusped roofs, creating an unmistakable profile that stands out against the blue sky. The surrounding gardens, well maintained and lush, offer an excellent opportunity for a relaxing walk, surrounded by colorful flowers and ancient trees.

Once you enter the castle, you will find yourself immersed in an atmosphere that tells centuries of history. The interiors have been lovingly restored and feature a collection of historical artifacts, period furnishings, and artworks that reflect Slovakia's rich cultural heritage. Each room tells a story, from the reception rooms, where large banquets and ceremonies once took place, to the private rooms of the nobles. The walls are decorated with frescoes that capture significant historical moments, allowing visitors to fully immerse themselves in the court life of yesteryear.

One of the most fascinating aspects of Bratislava Castle is its ability to adapt to change. Throughout history, the castle has suffered devastation, but it has always been rebuilt, testifying to the determination of the Slovak people to preserve their heritage. During the Austro-Hungarian period, the castle became a political and cultural center of great importance, hosting important meetings and conferences. Today, the castle is home to the Slovak National Museum, where visitors can learn about Slovakia's traditions, customs, and history through interactive and engaging exhibits.

As you explore the various rooms of the castle, it is impossible not to be impressed by the spectacular view that can be admired from its windows. The Danube River flows placidly at the foot of the hill, while the panorama of the city of Bratislava stretches to the horizon, with its historic buildings and modern structures coexisting in perfect harmony. Especially at sunset, when the sun tints the sky with golden and red shades, the view becomes simply enchanting, giving moments of pure magic.

Outside the castle, history lovers can also discover the ancient walls that once protected the fortification, walking along the paths that surround the site. These routes offer a unique opportunity to explore the remains of the ancient fortifications and appreciate the engineering work that has allowed the castle to withstand the wear and tear of time. Visitors can also stop at one of the many viewpoints, where you can admire the Danube and the surrounding hills, creating a perfect backdrop for unforgettable photographs.

Bratislava Castle is not only a place of historical interest, but also a centre for cultural events and artistic events. Throughout the year, the castle hosts concerts, festivals, and art exhibitions that attract artists and spectators from all over the world. These events offer an excellent opportunity to immerse yourself in the vibrant Slovak cultural scene and appreciate the creativity and talent of local artists.

An aspect that further enriches the visit to the castle is the possibility of participating in guided tours conducted by historical experts. These visits offer a unique opportunity to learn more about the history of the castle and the city as a whole. The passionate and knowledgeable guides share fascinating anecdotes and little-known details, making the experience even more engaging and educational.

For those who wish to deepen their experience at Bratislava Castle, it is also possible to participate in workshops and hands-on activities, where visitors can learn ancient craft techniques and discover the secrets of Slovak tradition. These interactive experiences are especially popular with families, as they offer a fun and engaging way to learn and discover local history.

Slovak gastronomy is another aspect that cannot be overlooked during a visit to the castle. In the immediate vicinity, there are numerous restaurants and cafes offering typical Slovak cuisine. Enjoying a traditional bryndzové halušky, potato dumplings served with sheep's cheese and bacon, or a local dessert such as trdelník, a kind of spiral cake baked on a wooden roller, is an experience that perfectly complements a visit to the castle. In addition, many of these establishments boast panoramic terraces that offer enchanting views of the castle itself and the city.

Visiting it in different seasons offers unique and evocative experiences. In spring, the gardens are filled with colors and scents, while summer brings with it outdoor events and concerts that liven up the atmosphere. Autumn offers warm and golden tones, while winter transforms the castle into an enchanting Christmas setting, with markets and decorations that create a magical atmosphere.

To get to Bratislava Castle, visitors can use public transport, which offers convenient and frequent connections to the city center. A walk from the Old Town to the castle is a pleasant option, as it allows you to discover the picturesque streets and hidden corners of Bratislava. In addition, the castle is also easily accessible for those traveling by car, with parking nearby.

In summary, Bratislava Castle is a must-see for anyone visiting Slovakia. Its fascinating history, architectural beauty and extraordinary views make this place a true jewel in the heart of Central Europe. Whether you're a history buff, a nature lover, or a curious traveler, the castle will win the hearts of anyone who sets foot there, leaving an indelible imprint on every visitor's memories.

Chapter 18: Bratislava Castle

Bratislava Castle, imposing and fascinating, is one of the most visited destinations in Slovakia, attracting thousands of tourists from all corners of the world every year. Located on a hill overlooking the Slovak capital, the castle is not only a symbol of the city, but also a silent witness to its troubled history, transformations and resilience. Its strategic location offers panoramic views of the Danube, Bratislava's Old Town, and even the distant Carpati Mountains, making the castle a must-see place for those looking to immerse themselves in the culture and history of this fascinating nation.

The castle's structure features four corner towers that rise majestic, each with its own distinctive design. The northern tower, the tallest, houses a bell tower that plays melodies that resonate throughout the city. The white walls of the castle sparkle in the sun, while the ancient stones tell stories of times gone by. Legend has it that the castle was initially built as a fortress by the Celts, but over the centuries it has undergone numerous alterations and expansions, until it became the residence of the Hungarian kings and nobles of the region.

Upon entering the castle, visitors are greeted by a large central courtyard, surrounded by historic buildings that house museums and art galleries. These exhibition spaces offer a rich overview of the history of Slovakia, from prehistoric times to the present day. Among the most notable pieces is an extensive collection of medieval artifacts, armor, and weapons, which chronicle daily life and the battles that took place in this region. Every corner of the castle is imbued with stories waiting to be discovered, and visitors can easily spend hours exploring its rooms and corridors.

The architecture of the castle is a remarkable example of the Baroque style, with Gothic and Renaissance influences that are harmoniously intertwined. The arched windows and carved decorations on the walls give the castle an air of nobility and grandeur. But what is most striking is the garden surrounding the castle, an ideal place for quiet walks and moments of reflection. The paved paths wind through colorful flower beds and centuries-old trees, creating a serene environment that contrasts with the hustle and bustle of urban life. The gardens also offer several benches where visitors can sit and enjoy the view of the Danube, which flows placidly below the castle walls.

One of the most fascinating aspects of Bratislava Castle is its tumultuous history. Over the centuries, the castle has been destroyed and rebuilt several times due to wars and invasions. Its last major renovation took place in the 50s of the twentieth century, when the communist government decided to restore it in order to turn it into a symbol of Slovak revival. This intervention has preserved the original structure, while adding modern elements that make it even more fascinating to visit.

Inside the castle is the Slovak National Museum, which offers a wide range of exhibits dedicated to Slovak history and culture. Here, visitors can admire a variety of art objects, traditional costumes, and musical instruments, reflecting the country's rich cultural heritage. The exhibits are carefully curated and provide an excellent opportunity to learn more about the life and traditions of the peoples who have inhabited this land over the centuries.

Bratislava Castle is also a venue for cultural events and events. Throughout the year, the castle hosts concerts, festivals, and historical reenactments that involve both residents and tourists. These events offer a unique opportunity to immerse yourself in Slovak culture and to better understand local traditions and customs. It is not uncommon to see groups of dancers in traditional costume performing in the courtyard of the castle, while musicians play melodies that resonate in the air, creating a festive and engaging atmosphere.

Another element that makes Bratislava Castle so fascinating is its accessibility. Located within walking distance of the city center, it is easily accessible on foot, giving visitors the chance to explore Bratislava's quaint narrow streets along the way. Once you get to the top, the panoramic view is worth every effort. The Danube winds like a blue ribbon, sailboats ply its calm waters, while the surrounding hills offer a breathtaking panorama. On a clear day, you can see all the way across the border, all the way to Austria.

In the evening, the castle lights up, creating a romantic and magical atmosphere. Soft lighting highlights the impressive architecture and gives visitors an enchanting panorama of the illuminated city. It is the ideal time to take unforgettable photographs and to enjoy a moment of tranquility as the day draws to a close.

A visit to Bratislava Castle would not be complete without a taste of the local gastronomy. Many restaurants and cafes nearby offer traditional Slovak dishes that can be enjoyed after a day of exploring. Specialties such as bryndzové halušky, a potato dumpling served with sheep's cheese, or kapustnica, a sauerkraut soup, are just some of the delights that visitors can try. These dishes, prepared according to traditional recipes, offer an extra layer of immersion in Slovak culture.

For those who wish to extend their stay, there are several accommodation options in the vicinity of the castle. From stylish boutique hotels to budget-friendly hostels, Bratislava offers accommodations for every type of traveler. Many of these places are located near the main tourist attractions, allowing you to explore the city with ease.

In summary, Bratislava Castle is much more than just a historical monument. It is a meeting place between past and present, a symbol of national identity and a reference point for Slovak culture. Its architectural beauty, cultural displays, and prime location make it one of the most fascinating destinations not only in Slovakia, but in all of Europe. Visitors who venture into this magical place can expect to return home with lasting memories and a new understanding of Slovak history and culture.

Chapter 19: Traditional Dishes and Gastronomic Culture of Slovakia

Slovakia, nestled in the heart of Central Europe, offers a rich and varied culinary landscape, the result of historical, geographical and cultural influences. Slovak cuisine is a fusion of ancient traditions and modernity, with dishes that tell the story of the people who have inhabited these lands. In this chapter, we will dive into the world of Slovak flavors, exploring the traditional dishes, local ingredients, and culinary habits that characterize this fascinating nation.

The basis of Slovak cuisine is simple but nutritious ingredients, such as potatoes, cereals, meat and dairy products. The dishes are often hearty and prepared using traditional methods that date back centuries. Slovak families gather around laden tables, where food is not only nourishment, but also a moment of sharing and conviviality.

One of the most iconic dishes of Slovakia is undoubtedly bryndzové halušky, potato dumplings topped with bryndza, a sheep's cheese typical of the region. This dish is considered the symbol of Slovak cuisine and is often served with smoked bacon or fried onion. The preparation of halušky is a real ritual: the potatoes are grated, mixed with flour and then cooked in boiling water until they become soft and delicate. The bryndza, with its intense and creamy flavor, blends perfectly with the gnocchi, creating a unique taste experience. Each bite tells stories of tradition and passion, making this dish a must-have for anyone visiting Slovakia.

Another traditional dish is kapustnica, a sauerkraut soup that varies from region to region. Ingredients can include smoked meat, dried mushrooms, and spices, making each recipe unique. During the holidays, kapustnica becomes a symbolic dish, often served at Christmas banquets. Its preparation takes time and dedication, as sauerkraut must be cooked slowly to develop a rich and complex flavor. Kapustnica is a perfect example of how Slovak cuisine values local products and family traditions.

Meat plays a central role in the Slovak diet, with pork, beef, and poultry dishes dominating the tables. Pečené mäso, roasted meat, is another traditional dish that cannot be missed. Often marinated with herbs and spices, the meat is slowly cooked until tender and succulent. This dish is usually accompanied by side dishes such as roasted potatoes, red cabbage, or mashed potatoes, creating a hearty and fulfilling meal. During the festivities and celebrations, pečené mäso is the protagonist, uniting families in a moment of joy and sharing.

Another fascinating aspect of Slovak gastronomy is its pastry. Slovak desserts are often made from simple ingredients, but their variety is amazing. Among the most well-known desserts is the trdelník, a tube-shaped cake baked on a wooden roller and sprinkled with sugar and nuts. Originally from the Transcarpathian region, it has become a symbol of Slovak cuisine and can be found at many fairs and markets. Its crunchiness on the outside and the softness on the inside make it irresistible, a sweet temptation to savor while walking through the streets of Slovak cities.

You can't talk about Slovak cuisine without mentioning the importance of drinks. Slovakia is famous for its brewing, with numerous microbreweries offering a wide range of craft beers. Slovak beer is often characterized by a rich taste and high quality, the result of a brewing tradition that dates back centuries. Another typical drink is borovička, a juniper-based liqueur that is consumed as an aperitif or digestive. This spirit, with its strong and aromatic flavor, is a symbol of Slovak culture and is often offered to guests as a sign of hospitality.

Slovak gastronomic culture is also deeply linked to local holidays and traditions. During the celebrations, specific dishes are prepared with great care, reflecting the practices and beliefs of the different regions. For example, during Easter, it is common to prepare a dessert called paska, a sweet bread enriched with eggs and raisins, a symbol of rebirth and prosperity. Each family has its own recipe, passed down from generation to generation, creating a sense of identity and cultural continuity.

In Slovakia, food is also a way to keep traditions alive. Many traditional dishes are prepared during festivals and festivals, events that celebrate local cuisine and regional specialties. During these events, you can savor a wide range of dishes, participate in cooking workshops and discover the story behind each recipe. It is a unique opportunity to immerse yourself in Slovak culture and to appreciate the culinary art that characterizes the country.

Slovakia is also a country of culinary contrasts, where influences from neighboring cultures, such as Hungarian, Austrian, and Czech, mix to create unique dishes. Paprika, for example, is a widely used ingredient in Slovak cuisine, especially in meat dishes. This spice not only gives color and flavor, but also represents a link to Hungarian cuisine, from which Slovakia has absorbed many culinary traditions.

Finally, it is important to note how Slovak gastronomy has been evolving in recent years. With the rise of interest in local and sustainable cuisine, many Slovak chefs are rediscovering traditional ingredients and cooking techniques, reinterpreting classic dishes in a modern way. Restaurants and trattorias offer menus that use fresh and local products, promoting a conscious approach to cooking. This renewed interest in Slovak gastronomy not only preserves tradition, but reinvents it, making it accessible to the new generations as well.

Thus, Slovakia presents itself as a fascinating gastronomic destination, where every dish tells a story and every flavor is an invitation to discover the roots of a rich and varied culture. Visitors will have the opportunity to explore local markets, participate in cooking classes, and enjoy traditional dishes in restaurants and trattorias, enjoying a culinary experience that goes beyond the simple act of eating. Slovak cuisine is a journey through flavors, a celebration of history and community, an unforgettable experience for anyone looking to immerse themselves in the culture of this beautiful country.

Chapter 20: Outdoor Activities in Slovakia

Slovakia is a true paradise for lovers of outdoor activities. With its breathtaking landscapes, mountain ranges, and crystal-clear waters, it offers a wide range of opportunities for those seeking adventures in the midst of nature. From hiking in the Tatra Alps to thrilling water experiences in rivers and lakes, to more extreme adventure activities, Slovakia has something for every type of traveler.

The Tatra Alps, part of the Carpathian mountain range, represent one of the most iconic places for trekking. The well-marked trails lead through spectacular landscapes, where you can admire imposing peaks, alpine lakes and unique flora and fauna. Some of the most famous routes include the trail that leads to Lake Štrbské Pleso, one of the most beautiful glacial lakes in Slovakia, and the trail that leads to the summit of Mount Rysy, the highest peak in Slovakia, which offers unforgettable views. During the summer season, these areas fill up with hikers, but also during the fall and winter, the region attracts visitors thanks to the warm colors of the leaves and the opportunities for skiing and snowboarding.

Another hotspot for trekking lovers is the Slovak Paradise National Park, a protected area that offers an abundance of trails that wind through deep gorges, waterfalls, and lush forests. Here, hikers can try their hand at more challenging routes, such as the famous trail that leads to the PRÍKRA waterfall. In addition, the park is known for its system of stairs and bridges that allow you to explore the most inaccessible areas, making the experience even more adventurous.

For those who love water activities, Slovakia does not disappoint. Slovak rivers, such as the Váh and Hron, are ideal for rafting and kayaking. In particular, the Váh River, the longest in the country, offers stretches suitable for both beginners and experts. Local agencies organize rafting tours that wind through spectacular scenery, with exciting rapids and calm waters where you can enjoy a break and admire the surrounding landscape. Kayaking and canoeing are equally popular, and many enthusiasts choose to explore the rivers on their own, renting the necessary equipment.

Water activities are not limited to rivers. Slovakia is dotted with lakes, many of which are perfect for swimming, windsurfing, or just relaxing on the shore. Zemplínska Šírava Lake, located in the eastern part of the country, is one of the largest and offers many opportunities for water sports. Not far away is Lake Štrbské Pleso, which is ideal for swimming in the summer months and ice skating in the winter. In addition, many lakes are surrounded by equipped beaches, where guests can rent pedal boats or simply enjoy a sunny day.

Slovakia is also a great place for mountain bikers. The mountains and hills offer a network of trails that vary in difficulty, making the area accessible to both beginners and experienced cyclists. One of the most renowned areas for mountain biking is the Malá Fatra region, with its scenic trails and exciting descents. Enthusiasts can rent bikes at various rental centers and take part in guided tours that combine a love of nature with the thrill of cycling.

Those looking for a little extra adrenaline can try paragliding, an activity that is gaining more and more popularity in Slovakia. The Tatra Alps offer some of the best paragliding launch points in Europe, with spectacular views and the chance to fly over towering peaks and verdant valleys. Several paragliding schools offer beginner courses and tandem flights with experienced instructors, making this experience accessible even to those who have never flown before.

Slovakia is also a great place for climbing. The limestone walls of the mountains offer challenges for climbers of all levels, from easy rock for beginners to more technical routes for experts. Popular climbing areas include Slovenský Raj National Park, known for its unique rock formations and spectacular trails, and Veľká Fatra National Park, which offers climbing opportunities in stunning scenery.

For those who are passionate about exploration, Slovakia is dotted with fascinating caves, many of which are open to the public. The Dobšinská Cave, a UNESCO World Heritage Site, is one of the most impressive and offers guided tours that allow you to admire stalactites and stalagmites of incredible beauty. Other caves, such as the Demänovská Cave, offer unique experiences, combining underground exploration with the natural beauty of the surrounding landscape.

Slovakia is also an excellent starting point for lovers of horseback riding. Several farms and equestrian centers offer tours that allow you to explore the Slovak countryside on horseback, with routes that wind through forests, grasslands, and valleys. Horse hikers can enjoy a unique experience, getting in touch with nature and discovering hidden corners of the country.

In every corner of Slovakia, you can find events and festivals related to nature and adventure. During the summer, numerous sports festivals take place throughout the country, offering rafting competitions, mountain biking courses, and even climbing events. These events not only offer the chance to watch exciting competitions, but also to meet other outdoor sports enthusiasts and share experiences.

The winter season brings with it a new dimension of outdoor adventures. The Tatra Alps become a center for winter sports, with renowned ski resorts such as Jasná and Tatranská Lomnica, offering slopes for skiers of all levels. Snowboarders can find rugged terrain and equipped parks, while cross-country skiing enthusiasts can explore miles of trails through enchanting scenery. There is no shortage of opportunities for snowshoeing, which allow you to immerse yourself in the winter tranquility of nature.

Slovakia is a country that invites you to discover and experience nature in all its forms. Whether it's climbing a mountain, cruising a river, cycling through woods, or simply strolling along a scenic trail, every outdoor activity offers the opportunity to immerse yourself in the natural beauty of this fascinating country. With such a wide variety of adventures, Slovakia is confirmed as one of the most promising European destinations for outdoor and adventure lovers.

Chapter 21: Cultural Experiences: Festivals, Local Events and Cultural Workshops in Slovakia

———

Slovakia, with its rich history and vibrant traditions, is a country where culture manifests itself in a myriad of forms, from folk celebrations to craft markets, to creative workshops that offer the opportunity to immerse yourself in local traditions. Every year, thousands of visitors join residents in lively and engaging festivities that tell stories of a people proud of their roots. This chapter explores the cultural experiences that make Slovakia a unique place, full of events that reflect the soul of its people.

Each season in Slovakia brings with it a series of festivals that celebrate music, art, and culinary traditions. Spring is the beginning of a time of rebirth and celebration. One of the most anticipated events is the Bratislava Spring Festival, which takes place in May. This festival transforms the center of the capital into a stage of art and culture, with concerts, dance performances and art exhibitions that attract artists and visitors from all over the world. The streets come alive with musicians of all genres, from the sounds of jazz to the melodies of classical music, creating a festive atmosphere that invites participation.

During this time, you can't miss the spring market, where local producers exhibit their handicrafts and gastronomic products. Visitors can savor local delicacies, such as "bryndzové halušky", a traditional dish made with potato dumplings and sheep's cheese. This is the ideal time to mingle with the locals and discover the stories related to the products you buy.

With the arrival of summer, Slovakia is transformed into a stage for internationally renowned music festivals. The Pohoda Music Festival, held in Trenčín, is one of the most significant events of the summer. This festival attracts world-renowned artists and a young and vibrant audience. The music ranges from rock to electronic, with performances taking place on multiple stages. What makes Pohoda special is not only the music, but also the community atmosphere that is created among the participants, combined with a strong sense of sustainability and respect for the environment.

Parallel to these musical events, local holidays offer an authentic glimpse into everyday life in Slovakia. The feast of St. Michael, which is celebrated in September, is a perfect example of how religious and cultural traditions intertwine. In several locations, processions and fairs are held in honor of the saint, where you can taste typical sweets and attend folk shows. The inhabitants wear traditional costumes and dance to the rhythm of folk songs, offering visitors a unique and immersive experience.

Slovakia is also famous for its wine festivals, which celebrate the country's winemaking tradition. The Tokaj region, in particular, is known for its sweet wines and artisanal winemaking. Every year in September, the Tokaj Wine Festival is organized, where local producers present their best labels. Visitors can participate in tastings, learn winemaking techniques, and enjoy live concerts that accompany the celebration. This festival is not only an opportunity to taste fine wines, but also to immerse yourself in the local culture and meet the producers who passionately tell about their work.

Autumn brings with it another series of cultural events, including the Bratislava International Film Festival. This festival attracts cinephiles and industry professionals from all over the world, presenting a selection of independent films and feature debuts. In addition to screenings, debates and meetings with directors and actors take place, creating an atmosphere of cultural and artistic exchange. This event is an important platform for Slovak cinema, which has seen significant growth in recent years, helping to introduce Slovak culture to an international audience.

In winter, Slovakia turns into a fairytale country, and the Christmas festivities are a special time to experience the local culture. Towns and villages are filled with Christmas markets, where you can buy local handicrafts, Christmas decorations, and culinary delights. Bratislava's markets, in particular, are famous for their enchanting atmosphere, with twinkling lights and the scents of mulled wine and traditional sweets. Christmas events culminate with the celebration of Christmas Eve, when families come together to share typical dishes and traditions that are passed down from generation to generation.

In addition to festivals, Slovakia offers a variety of cultural workshops that allow visitors to immerse themselves in different forms of art and tradition. These workshops are a unique opportunity to learn directly from local artists and artisans, who share their techniques and stories. Pottery workshops, for example, are very popular and take place in different cities, where participants can create their own works of art under the expert guidance of master potters. These moments of creativity not only allow you to take home a unique piece, but also offer an authentic and personal experience of Slovak culture.

Another significant workshop is the one dedicated to traditional music. In different regions, you can participate in folk dance and folk music classes, where you can learn the dance steps and melodies typical of Slovakia. These workshops are a way to connect with the local community and better understand the traditions that underpin Slovak culture.

In some cities, such as Košice and Nitra, cultural events are held that celebrate contemporary art. The art galleries and exhibition spaces host exhibitions by local and international artists, creating a dialogue between tradition and modernity. These events offer the opportunity to discover new talents and immerse yourself in the Slovak art scene, which is constantly evolving.

Slovakia, with its rich variety of festivals, events and cultural workshops, is a real treasure trove of authentic experiences. Each event is an invitation to discover the traditions and stories that make this country so special. Whether dancing to traditional music, enjoying typical dishes, or creating a work of art, each experience offers a unique opportunity to connect with Slovak culture and the people who live it. Visitors can thus take home not only souvenirs, but also indelible memories of a journey that enriches the soul.

Chapter 22: Itinerary for an unforgettable day in Bratislava

Bratislava, the capital of Slovakia, is a city that enchants with its history, architecture and vibrant culture. Located on the banks of the Danube, just a stone's throw from the borders of Austria and Hungary, Bratislava is a crossroads of cultures and traditions. A day here may seem insufficient, but with a careful travel plan, it is possible to grasp the essence of the city and discover its most fascinating corners.

We start our day in the beating heart of Bratislava, the Main Square, or Hlavné námestie. This is the ideal place to start your adventure. Surrounded by majestic historic buildings, the square is a lively meeting point for locals and tourists alike. Admire the façade of the Old Town Hall, a Gothic building that dates back to the thirteenth century, with its distinctive tower and charming decorations. Take a moment to observe the rhythm of city life: outdoor cafes begin to fill with people sipping coffee and chatting, while seasonal markets often enliven the square.

From here, head to Bratislava Castle, which towers over the city with its impressive white structure. The walk up to the castle is a short but pleasant hike. Along the way, you may come across charming souvenir shops and art galleries. Once you reach the castle, prepare to be surprised by the panoramic view it offers over the city and the Danube. The architecture of the castle, with its towers and imposing walls, tells stories of a rich and turbulent past. Inside, the Slovak National Museum offers an overview of Slovakia's history, with exhibits ranging from ancient art to medieval artifacts.

After exploring the castle, it's time to immerse yourself in Slovak food culture. Head down to the Old Town and indulge in lunch at one of the traditional restaurants. The typical dish to try is halušky, potato dumplings served with sheep's cheese and smoked bacon. Accompany your meal with a local beer, such as Zlatý Bažant, for an authentic experience. As you enjoy your lunch, take the time to observe the details of the restaurant's interior, often decorated with folkloric elements that reflect Slovak cultural identity.

After lunch, it's time to discover the charm of the old town. As you stroll through the narrow cobbled streets, you will come across several architectural wonders. Don't miss St. Martin's Church, a Gothic jewel that preserves St. Stephen's crown, a symbol of the Hungarian kingdom. Continuing your walk, you will have the opportunity to meet the famous Man at Work, a sculpture representing a worker in a manhole, an icon of the city. Local artists have created a lively and creative atmosphere, and you may even discover contemporary art galleries along the way.

Your next stop will be the Grassalkovich Palace, the official residence of the President of Slovakia. Although it is not possible to enter, the surrounding gardens are worth a visit. Here, you can stroll through flower beds and fountains, enjoying a quiet moment away from the hustle and bustle of the city. Take some photos and admire the neoclassical architecture of the palace, which shines in the sun.

Towards the afternoon, head towards the Danube. A walk along the river is a must. The riverfront is buzzing with street performers and outdoor cafes, where you can stop to enjoy ice cream or fresh lemonade. If you're feeling adventurous, consider renting a bike and riding the riverside trails. The view of the flowing water and the surrounding hills is simply breathtaking. You could also opt for a Danube River cruise, which offers a unique perspective on the city and its panorama.

As the sun begins to set, it's time to discover one of Bratislava's most vibrant neighborhoods: the Petržalka district. Known for its communist architecture and large residential complexes, this neighborhood offers an interesting contrast to the historic center. Here, you can explore the local markets and savor typical snacks, such as trdlo, yeast dough sweets rolled in sugar and cinnamon. Life here is hectic, and you can easily feel the young and dynamic atmosphere that characterizes this neighborhood.

As the evening approaches, head back to the center to experience the nighttime energy of Bratislava. The city offers a wide range of dining options, from fine dining to casual dining. If you want a unique dining experience, book a table at one of the restaurants overlooking the Danube. Here, you can enjoy typical Slovak dishes prepared with fresh, local ingredients, all while taking in the enchanting panorama of the illuminated city.

After dinner, you can't miss a walk along the Danube. The lights of the city reflect on the water, creating a romantic and atmospheric atmosphere. You may also discover cultural events or outdoor concerts taking place along the river, making your experience even more memorable. If you're a history buff, consider visiting the Bratislava City Museum, which often hosts evening exhibitions on historical and cultural themes.

To end your day, choose one of the city's historic bars for a drink. Bratislava's cafes and bars are known for their cozy atmosphere and friendly service. Try a cocktail made with slivovitz, the famous Slovakian plum liqueur, or a glass of local wine, which will allow you to savor the flavors of the region. Listen to live music or simply enjoy conversation with locals, who are often happy to share stories and tips on how to best explore their beloved city.

When night falls on Bratislava, you're sure to have accumulated unmissable memories and a deep appreciation for this fascinating capital city. Every corner of the city tells a story, and one day is never enough to discover all that Bratislava has to offer. However, with this itinerary, you had the opportunity to savor the beauty and peculiarities of one of the most fascinating cities in Europe, leaving you with a desire to return to explore further and immerse yourself in its rich culture and history.

Chapter 23: Three-Day Itinerary in Slovakia

Slovakia, with its stunning landscapes, historic cities, and rich culture, is an ideal destination for a short getaway. This three-day itinerary will take you to discover the wonders of this fascinating country, from the dynamism of its cities to the serenity of its mountains, allowing you to fully immerse yourself in Slovak life.

The first day begins in Bratislava, the country's capital, a city that combines millennia-old history with a vibrant, modern atmosphere. You should start your day by exploring the Old Town, a maze of narrow cobbled streets, vibrant squares, and charming architecture. Head to Bratislava Castle, located on a hill overlooking the city and the Danube River. From here, you can enjoy a panoramic view that embraces the city and its surroundings. The castle itself is an architectural gem, with a history dating back to the ninth century. After your visit, head down to the center and treat yourself to a coffee at one of the many historic cafes that dot the main square.

In the afternoon, visit the Church of San Martino, known for its colorful tile roof. This Gothic church has witnessed numerous historical events, including the coronations of Hungarian kings. Continuing on, don't miss the Grassalkovich Palace, the current residence of the Slovak president, surrounded by beautiful gardens. The day ends with a walk along the Danube, where you can admire the UFO Bridge, an icon of Bratislava. For dinner, I recommend you try typical Slovak cuisine in one of the traditional restaurants, enjoying dishes such as bryndzové halušky, potato dumplings with sheep's cheese.

The second day will take you to the heart of Slovak nature, in the Tatra National Park. After a hearty breakfast, take a train from Bratislava to Poprad, a small town that serves as a gateway to the mountains. Once you arrive, head to the village of Štrbské Pleso, famous for its lake and spectacular views. Here you can take a walk along the lake or, if you are an adventure lover, try some of the hikes that start from this point. The high peaks of the Tatras offer routes of varying difficulty, suitable for both beginners and experienced hikers.

In the afternoon, visit the center of Tatranská Lomnica, another picturesque mountain village. Here you will have the chance to take a cable car to the top of the Lomnický štít mountain, which offers indescribable views. Don't forget to bring a camera with you, as the landscapes are unique and unforgettable. After a day full of outdoor activities, return to Poprad and indulge in dinner at a local restaurant, where you can savor meat dishes and fresh cheeses.

The third day is dedicated to discovering Slovak history and culture. Start your day by visiting Spiš Castle, one of the largest castles in Europe, located on a hill overlooking the valley below. Its history dates back to the thirteenth century and today it is a UNESCO World Heritage Site. Explore the castle ruins and enjoy the spectacular view that stretches to the horizon. The interior, although in ruins, tells stories of nobles and warriors who inhabited these lands.

After exploring the castle, head to the town of Levoča, famous for its well-preserved old town and the Church of St. James, which houses an impressive wooden sculpture from the 14th century. Stroll through the cobblestone streets and let yourself be carried away by the magic of this place. Don't forget to savor a typical dessert of the area, the trdelník, a spiral dessert cooked on the grill and sprinkled with sugar.

The afternoon is perfect for visiting the city of Košice, the second largest city in Slovakia. Here, St. Elizabeth's Cathedral, a stunning example of Gothic architecture, will leave you speechless. Explore the main square, which is a vibrant center of culture and city life. You can also visit the National Theatre and the Museum of Contemporary Art, which offer an in-depth insight into the Slovak art scene.

For your last dinner in Slovakia, choose a restaurant that offers traditional dishes. Take advantage of this opportunity to reflect on the experiences you have lived and the places you have discovered. Slovakia, with its combination of history, culture, and nature, is sure to leave you with lasting memories.

This three-day itinerary is just a taste of the wonders that Slovakia has to offer. Every corner of this country tells a story, and it is only by traveling and discovering that you will be able to fully understand the beauty and diversity of this fascinating land.

Chapter 24: 5 Days Itinerary in Slovakia

———

S lovakia, a charming country located in the heart of Central Europe, offers a unique combination of natural beauty, fascinating history, and vibrant culture. This five-day itinerary will take you to discover the wonders of Slovakia, from mountains to castles, from historic towns to traditional gastronomy. Get ready to immerse yourself in an unforgettable journey through this land full of surprises.

Start your adventure in the capital, Bratislava, a city overlooking the Danube River that is characterized by a mix of modern and ancient architecture. When you arrive, settle into one of the many hotels in the historic center, where you can easily get around on foot. After freshening up, begin your exploration with a stroll through the old town, known as Staré Mesto. Here, you can admire the majestic Bratislava Castle, which dominates the city from the top of a hill. Don't miss the chance to visit St. Martin's Cathedral, a Gothic masterpiece that hosts the coronation ceremonies of Hungarian kings.

In the afternoon, head to the New Bridge, a symbol of the city that offers spectacular panoramic views of the Danube and the castle. Continuing on, you can stop at the Hlavné Námestie market, where you can savor local specialties, such as bryndzové halušky, potato dumplings with sheep's cheese. In the evening, enjoy dinner in one of the typical restaurants, where you can savor traditional dishes and good Slovak wine.

On the second day, take a train or bus to the picturesque town of Trnava, known as the "Slovak Rome" for its number of churches. Here you can visit the Basilica of San Nicola and stroll through the cobbled streets of the historic center. Don't forget to taste the typical dessert of the area, trnavská štrúdľa, a delicious apple pie. After exploring Trnava, continue your journey to Nitra, one of the oldest cities in Slovakia. Visit Nitra Castle, which offers stunning views of the city and the surrounding hills. The day ends with dinner at a local restaurant, where you can enjoy meat dishes and seasonal side dishes.

On the third day, it's time to venture out into nature. Head to the Tatra National Park, a true paradise for outdoor enthusiasts. Choose a trail that suits your level of experience and immerse yourself in the breathtaking landscapes of the mountains. Lake Štrbské Pleso, with its crystal clear waters and mountains in the background, is a must-see destination. If you're in the mood for a more challenging hike, consider climbing Mount Gerlach, Slovakia's highest peak. After a day of adventure, relax in one of the mountain huts, where you can savor typical dishes such as pirohy, ravioli stuffed with potatoes or meat.

On the fourth day, after a hearty breakfast, head to the UNESCO-listed town of Banská Štiavnica. This historic mining town is famous for its Baroque architecture and picturesque squares. Visit the Museum of Mining and Banská Štiavnica Castle, where you can enjoy panoramic views of the city. Don't waste time exploring the botanical garden and surrounding lakes, ideal for a relaxing stroll. In the evening, treat yourself to dinner at one of the local restaurants, where you can try the secret of traditional Banská Štiavnica recipes.

On the fifth day, return to Bratislava for one last exploration. Visit the Slovak National Museum and the Bratislava City Museum, where you can delve into the country's history and culture. If you're an art lover, don't miss the Museum of Contemporary Art, which houses works by Slovak and international artists. In the afternoon, take a boat ride on the Danube, a perfect way to admire the city from a different perspective. Conclude your Slovak adventure with dinner at a restaurant overlooking the river, where you can reflect on your experiences and plan your next trip.

Slovakia is a land of contrasts, where history is intertwined with modernity, and where natural beauty blends with culture. This five-day itinerary gives you a taste of the many facets of this fascinating country, leaving you with unforgettable memories and a desire to return.

Chapter 25: 7-Day Itinerary in Slovakia

Slovakia is a country that enchants with its natural beauty, rich history, and vibrant culture. This seven-day itinerary will guide you through the wonders of this Central European gem, offering you an authentic and unforgettable experience.

Your journey begins in the capital, Bratislava, a charming city located along the banks of the Danube. Once you arrive, take a moment to immerse yourself in the pulsating life of this city. Walking through the old town, the cobbled streets will lead you to discover Baroque and medieval architecture, with churches and palaces that tell stories of a fascinating past. Don't miss the view from Bratislava Castle, which rises majestically over the surrounding hills, offering a panoramic perspective of the city and the river. In the evening, treat yourself to dinner in one of the traditional restaurants, where you can enjoy typical dishes such as bryndzové halušky, potato dumplings with sheep's cheese and bacon.

The second day will take you to explore the stunning Tatra National Park. Departing from Bratislava, head to the town of Poprad, a great starting point for mountain hikes. From here, you can take a cable car to Hrebienok, where a network of trails begins that will take you to discover breathtaking landscapes. The hike to Lake Poprad is a must, a picturesque area where you can relax and enjoy the tranquility of nature. In the evening, return to Poprad to enjoy a local dinner, perhaps accompanied by a good Slovak wine.

On the third day, visit the town of Štrbské Pleso, another pearl of the Tatras. Here you can take a walk around the lake, surrounded by imposing mountains, and, if you are an adventure lover, you can try your hand at activities such as hiking or even cycling. Don't forget to visit St. Elizabeth's Church, an architectural gem made of wood. After a busy day, relax in one of the many spas in the area, where you can rejuvenate before continuing your journey.

The fourth day takes you to the historic town of Banská Štiavnica, recognized as a UNESCO World Heritage Site. This mining town is famous for its unique architecture and rich mining history. Walking through its narrow streets, you will discover cozy cafes and local craft shops. Visit the Museum of Mining and Banská Štiavnica Castle, where you can unravel the secrets of a bygone era. Don't forget to savor the typical dessert, trdelník, as you explore the city's squares and gardens.

On the fifth day, your journey will take you to Bratislava, where you will have the opportunity to immerse yourself in the cultural life of the capital. Visit the Primatial Palace, the seat of government, and St. Martin's Cathedral, a Gothic masterpiece. Take advantage of this day to take a boat ride on the Danube, enjoying a unique view of the city from the water. In the evening, head to the Petržalka district, where you can enjoy regional dishes in a lively atmosphere, with live music and warm hospitality.

Day six will take you to explore the Central Slovakia region, with a visit to Trenčín, famous for its medieval castle overlooking the city. Stroll through the streets of the center and visit the historic knights' hall. After a visit to the castle, head to the town of piešťany, famous for its hot springs. Here you can treat yourself to a wellness treatment, a perfect way to relax and recharge your batteries for the last days of your trip.

Finally, on day seven, get ready to discover Slovenský raj National Park, known for its spectacular trails that wind through gorges, waterfalls, and rock formations. This is the ideal place for lovers of nature and outdoor sports. You can hike along the famous Suchá Belá trail, with passages through wooden bridges and ladders that will take you to incredible views. After a day of adventure, head back to Bratislava for a farewell dinner at one of the riverside restaurants, where you can reflect on everything you've experienced during this unforgettable week.

Slovakia is a country that knows how to surprise and fascinate, with its mixture of history, culture and nature. This seven-day itinerary offers a taste of the wonders this nation has to offer, allowing you to create lasting memories and appreciate the warm hospitality of the Slovak people. End your trip with a heart full of experiences and an open mind to further adventures on your next trip.

Chapter 26: 10-Day Itinerary in Slovakia

Slovakia, a country nestled in the heart of Europe, is an often overlooked gem, but rich in history, culture, and stunning scenery. With a ten-day itinerary, you will have the opportunity to explore the vibrant cities, historic castles, and unspoiled nature that characterize this fascinating country. Get ready for an unforgettable journey that will take you through the most emblematic places and hidden gems of Slovakia.

The first day begins in the capital, Bratislava. This charming city, located on the banks of the Danube, is a perfect mix of modernity and tradition. A walk through the old town will take you to discover the beauty of the Main Square, with its colorful buildings and cozy cafes. Don't miss the opportunity to visit Bratislava Castle, which offers panoramic views of the city and the river. After a day of exploring, treat yourself to dinner in one of the typical restaurants, where you can enjoy traditional dishes such as bryndzové halušky, potato dumplings with sheep's cheese.

The second day is dedicated to discovering the natural wonders of the Tatras National Park. Departing from Bratislava, take a train or bus to the town of Poprad, the gateway to this beautiful mountainous area. Once there, head to Tatranská Lomnica, where you can embark on a scenic hike up to Mount Lomnicky. The stunning views of snow-capped peaks and green valleys will make your day unforgettable. At the end of the hike, return to Poprad for a relaxing dinner at one of the local restaurants.

On the third day, explore the charming towns of Štrbské Pleso and Starý Smokovec. These two mountain resorts offer trekking routes suitable for all skill levels. The beauty of Lake Štrbské Pleso, surrounded by beech and pine trees, is a great place for a relaxing walk or picnic. After spending the day outdoors, return to Poprad for an evening of rest, perhaps enjoying a Slovak craft beer.

The fourth day will take you to Košice, the second largest city in Slovakia. Starting from Poprad, the train journey will take you through picturesque landscapes. Once in Košice, visit St. Elizabeth's Cathedral, a magnificent example of Gothic architecture. Walking through the old town, let yourself be fascinated by the beauty of the main street and its lively atmosphere. Košice is also famous for its cultural festivals, so check the schedule of events during your visit.

On the fifth day, get ready for an adventure in Slava National Park, a protected area that is home to incredible flora and fauna. Here, you'll be able to explore hiking trails that will take you through lush forests and fascinating rock formations. Don't forget to visit Betliar Castle, an architectural marvel surrounded by lovely gardens. After a day spent in nature, return to Košice for a traditional dinner.

Day six will take you to Banská Štiavnica, one of the most beautiful and historic mining towns in Slovakia. This UNESCO-listed city is famous for its Baroque architecture and rich mining history. Visit the Mineral Museum and St. Catherine's Church to immerse yourself in local history. Don't forget to stroll along the picturesque paths that lead to the many artificial lakes in the area, perfect for relaxing and enjoying the tranquility of nature.

On day seven, head to Bratislava to explore the wine region of western Slovakia. Visit the town of Trnava, known for its baroque churches and well-preserved old town. Continue to the Pezinok Hills, where you can taste excellent local wines at one of the many wineries. Slovakia is famous for its white wines, so don't miss the chance to savor a fine wine while admiring the views of the vineyards.

The eighth day is dedicated to exploring Spiš Castle, one of the largest castles in Europe. Located on a hill, it offers spectacular views of the surrounding countryside and the town of Spišská Nová Ves. After visiting the castle, explore the charming towns of Levoča and Kežmarok, where you can admire the medieval architecture and savor the local cuisine.

Day nine will take you to the heart of Slovakia, to Žilina, a bustling town located near the Little Carpathian Mountains. Visit Budatín Castle and stroll along the Váh River. Take advantage of your stay to discover local traditions, perhaps by taking part in a pottery workshop or a Slovak cooking class. The city also offers a vibrant nightlife, so get ready to enjoy a drink at one of the bars in the center.

On the tenth day, conclude your trip in Bratislava, where you will have the opportunity to visit the Slovak National Museum and the Grassalkovich Palace, the official residence of the President of Slovakia. Relax in one of the city's parks, such as Sad Janka Kráľa Park, and enjoy your last evening savoring Slovak cuisine in a rooftop restaurant overlooking the Danube. Slovakia has a lot to offer, and this ten-day itinerary will allow you to savor a wide range of cultural, historical, and natural experiences.

Every day spent in Slovakia will give you unforgettable memories and the chance to immerse yourself in a rich and vibrant culture. With this itinerary, you will have experienced an authentic adventure, discovering the wonders of a country that deserves to be explored and appreciated. Slovakia is a place where history is intertwined with natural beauty, and every corner tells a story just waiting to be discovered.

Chapter 27: 14-Day Itinerary in Slovakia

S lovakia is an enchanting country in the heart of Europe, rich in history, culture and stunning scenery. In this chapter, we will present a 14-day itinerary that will allow you to explore the wonders of this fascinating country, from its historic cities to its national parks, to the castles that dot the territory. Every day will be an opportunity to discover something new and immerse yourself in warm Slovak hospitality.

Your journey begins in the capital, Bratislava, a bustling city overlooking the Danube River. Spend the first two days exploring the Old Town, which features cobbled streets, colorful buildings, and charming cafes. Don't miss the Bratislava Castle, which offers panoramic views of the city and the river. As you stroll through the squares, visit the Cathedral of San Martino and the Primatial Palace, where you can admire beautiful frescoes and works of art. For a taste of local culture, treat yourself to a typical dinner in a traditional restaurant, where you can enjoy dishes such as bryndzové halušky, potato dumplings with sheep's cheese.

On the third day, take a train north, towards Trenčín. This charming town is famous for its medieval castle, which stands on a hill and offers spectacular views. Spend the afternoon exploring the city center, where you'll find a combination of historic and modern architecture. Stop at the famous stone bridge and visit the church of St. Francis of Assisi. In the evening, enjoy an aperitif in one of the local bars, savoring a cold Slovak beer.

On the fourth day, continue your journey to Malá Fatra National Park. This area offers unspoiled nature, hiking trails and extraordinary views. You can choose to hike to the top of Mount Veľký Kriváň, where you'll be rewarded with spectacular views. After a day of outdoor adventures, relax in one of the mountain huts, where you can enjoy local dishes and recharge your batteries.

On the fifth day, move on to the town of Žilina, one of the most important in northern Slovakia. Learn about its history by visiting St. Paul's Church and Budatín Castle. Žilina is also a great starting point for exploring the surrounding mountains and stunning natural landscapes. If you have time, visit nearby Lake Teplá, an ideal destination for a walk or picnic.

On the sixth day, direct your path to the spectacular Demänovská Caves. These caves offer a unique experience, with stalactites and stalagmites creating a magical environment. After exploring the caves, continue to the nearby Nízké Tatry National Park, where you can go on a hike or simply enjoy the serenity of nature. In the evening, find accommodation in one of the mountain huts, where you can savor the local cuisine.

On the seventh day, continue your journey to the city of Poprad, gateway to the Tatras. From here, take the cable car to Lomnický Mountain, one of the highest peaks in this mountain range. Climb to the top and marvel at the panoramic view. Alternatively, explore the Tatra National Park, where you can hike trails that will take you to alpine lakes and waterfalls. In the evening, return to Poprad and enjoy its lively nightlife.

On day eight, take your time to discover the village of Štrbské Pleso, famous for its lake and outdoor activity opportunities. Here you can rent a bike or take a walk along the lake, enjoying the tranquility of the place. Don't forget to savor a coffee in one of the cafes overlooking the lake. After a day of relaxation, head to the town of Liptovský Mikuláš for another night.

Day nine will take you to Banská Bystrica, one of the most historic cities in Slovakia. Here you can visit the Museum of Central Slovakia and learn about the mining history of the region. Stroll through the city center, admiring the Baroque architecture and historic churches. In the evening, treat yourself to dinner in a restaurant offering local specialties, accompanied by a good Slovak wine.

On the tenth day, head south, to Slovenský raj National Park. This park is famous for its scenic trails and spectacular gorges. Dedicate the day to hiking, following the paths that will take you over suspension bridges and waterfalls. Your adventure in nature will be an unforgettable experience, and you can return to your accommodation in the evening to rest and reflect on the day.

On the eleventh day, visit the city of Košice, the second largest city in Slovakia. Explore the Old Town with its impressive St. Elizabeth's Cathedral and the main square. Košice is also a great place to savor modern Slovak cuisine in innovative restaurants. Don't forget to stroll along the Hornád River, where you can admire the cityscape and relax.

On day twelve, take a train to Spiš Castle, one of the largest castles in Europe and a UNESCO World Heritage Site. Explore the ruins and learn about the fascinating history of this place. After your visit to the castle, head to the town of Levoča, famous for its Church of St. James and the beautiful Gothic altar. Spend the night in this historic city, soaking up its unique atmosphere.

On the thirteenth day, explore the Tokaj wine region, on the border with Hungary. Here you can visit the cellars and taste some of the best wines in Slovakia. Join a guided tour to discover the secrets of wine production and savor local wines accompanied by gastronomic delicacies. The evening can end with a dinner in one of the traditional taverns in the area.

Finally, on the fourteenth day, head back to Bratislava for one last day of exploration. Visit museums you didn't get to see at the beginning of your trip, such as the Slovak National Museum or the Bratislava City Museum. Take advantage of this time to shop at the local markets and take home unique souvenirs. Conclude your Slovak adventure with dinner at a restaurant overlooking the Danube, reflecting on the wonderful experiences lived in this fascinating country.

This 14-day itinerary will take you through some of Slovakia's most iconic and fascinating sights, offering you a mix of culture, history, and natural beauty. Each day will be an opportunity to immerse yourself in Slovak life and discover the richness of a country that, despite being often overlooked, has a lot to offer curious travelers.

Chapter 28: The Best Tours and Excursions in Slovakia

Slovakia, with its stunning scenery and rich cultural history, offers endless opportunities for trips and excursions that go far beyond its charming cities. While Bratislava and Košice attract visitors with their historical monuments and vibrant nightlife, the real treasure of this country is often found outside its urban centers. In this chapter, we will explore some of the best day trips that reveal Slovakia's natural beauty, cultural heritage, and unique traditions.

One of the most iconic hikes is to the Tatri National Park, one of the most fascinating protected areas in Slovakia. Located on the border with Poland, the park is famous for its majestic peaks, crystal clear lakes and verdant valleys. Nature lovers will find countless trails that wind through spectacular landscapes. One of the most popular walks is the one that leads to Lake Štrbské Pleso, a great place for a picnic or just to enjoy the surrounding beauty. If you're looking for adventure, the trail to Mount Gerlach, the highest peak of the Tatris, offers a rewarding challenge and unforgettable views.

Continuing east, you cannot overlook the town of Banská Štiavnica, an old mining center declared a World Heritage Site by UNESCO. Its historic center is a maze of narrow cobbled streets, baroque palaces and historic churches. The city is also famous for its crater lakes, which provide opportunities for swimming and relaxing. A visit to the Mineral Museum and St. Catherine's Church is a must to understand the mining history of the region. Don't forget to savor the local cuisine in one of the traditional restaurants, where dishes such as "lokše", a kind of potato crepe, will immerse you in the Slovak gastronomic culture.

If you want a more authentic and rural experience, a trip to Čičmany is perfect. This village is known for its wooden houses decorated with traditional Slovak motifs. As you stroll through the narrow streets of Čičmany, you will be able to appreciate the local folk art and understand how the community preserves the traditions of the past. A visit to the Slovak Village Museum will allow you to learn more about Slovakian peasant life and customs. This is a place where time seems to have stopped, offering a serene atmosphere and a genuine connection to the past.

Another must-see destination is the city of Trnava, often nicknamed "Slovak Rome" due to its impressive number of churches and cathedrals. The historic center is dominated by the Cathedral of St. Nicholas, a masterpiece of the Baroque. Walking through the squares and cobbled streets, you can discover the charm of one of the oldest cities in Slovakia. Don't forget to visit the church of St. John the Baptist, which offers a mix of Gothic and Baroque architecture. Trnava is also famous for its wines; therefore, a stop at one of the local wineries for a wine tasting is highly recommended.

If you're a history buff, a visit to Spiš Castle is an experience not to be missed. Located on a hill overlooking the valley, this impressive castle is one of the largest castles in Central Europe. Its history dates back to the twelfth century and offers a fascinating glimpse into medieval life in Slovakia. The impressive architecture and breathtaking views from the top of the towers make this visit an unforgettable moment. The castle is surrounded by a protected natural area, so you can also explore the surrounding paths for a total immersion in nature.

Another trip that deserves attention is to Nitra, one of the oldest cities in Slovakia and an important cultural center. Nitra Castle, located on a hill, offers panoramic views of the city and houses a museum that tells the story of the region. The Cathedral of San Emerano, with its Romanesque and Baroque architecture, is another highlight to visit. Nitra is also known for its vibrant markets and folk traditions, making it a fascinating destination to discover Slovak culture.

If you want to immerse yourself in nature, the Suchá Belá Gorge in the Slovak Paradise National Park is a great choice. This hike is characterized by spectacular limestone formations, waterfalls, and trails that wind through dense forests. Walking through the gorge offers the chance to cross wooden bridges and stairs, making the experience even more adventurous. Photography lovers will find postcard landscapes here, with vibrant colors and dreamy scenery. It is a great place for a day of exploration, away from the hustle and bustle of city life.

For a more spiritual experience, a trip to the Jasov Monastery is highly recommended. This Benedictine monastery, located near Košice, is a place of peace and tranquility. The Baroque architecture and interior frescoes are absolutely fascinating. The monastery is surrounded by a beautiful park, where you can walk and relax. The visit also includes a walk near the Jasov Caves, a cave system that offers an interesting opportunity to explore the geology of the region.

If your adventure takes you to the western part of the country, don't miss the chance to visit Trenčín Castle. This historic fortress, located on a hill, is famous for its legends, including that of a beautiful princess. The castle offers guided tours that tell its history and strategic importance over the centuries. From the top of the castle, you can enjoy panoramic views of the city and the surrounding valley, a perfect place to take memorable photographs.

For a wellness outing, the town of Piešťany is renowned for its thermal springs and wellness centres. This spa town is famous for its healing treatments and modern facilities that attract visitors from all over the world. Spending a day here will allow you to relax and rejuvenate, taking advantage of the thermal waters and relaxing massages. The beauty of the surrounding parks and gardens makes the atmosphere even more pleasant.

Finally, for those who love wine, a visit to the vineyards of the Tokaj region is an experience not to be missed. This area, famous for its sweet wines, offers vineyard tours and tastings that allow you to discover the local varieties. Walking through the rows of vines, you can appreciate the beauty of the landscape while savoring a glass of fine wine. Historic cellars also offer a chance to learn about Slovakia's winemaking tradition and production techniques.

Every trip and excursion in Slovakia is an opportunity to discover the beauty of the country and its rich culture. Whether you're exploring the mountains, visiting historic castles, or immersing yourself in local traditions, Slovakia offers unforgettable experiences that will enrich your trip. The variety of landscapes and cultural diversity make each excursion unique, allowing you to discover hidden corners and fascinating stories. With careful planning, you can make the most of your time in Slovakia, creating treasured memories that will accompany your trip forever.

Chapter 29: Practical Information for a Trip to Slovakia

S lovakia, a charming country located in the heart of Europe, is a fascinating destination for travelers looking for breathtaking landscapes, rich culture, and living traditions. Before embarking on the trip, it is essential to gather some practical information that can make the experience smoother and more enjoyable. This chapter provides all the information you need, from documentation to transport, from safety to gastronomy, to help you plan your stay in Slovakia.

The documentation required to enter Slovakia is relatively simple. For citizens of the European Union, a valid ID is sufficient, while for travelers from non-EU countries, a valid passport is required. A short-stay visa is not required, but it is always advisable to check for any regulatory updates before departure. Since 2004, Slovakia has been part of the Schengen area, which means that once you cross the border, there will be no internal border controls. However, it is important to keep your documents handy in case they are required.

Once you arrive in Slovakia, you immediately realize that the transport network is well-developed and accessible. Major cities, such as Bratislava, Košice, Prešov and Nitra, are connected by an efficient bus and train network. The Slovenská pošta, the national railway agency, offers numerous connections that cover not only the main cities but also the rural areas, allowing travelers to discover the authenticity of the country. Trains are usually punctual and comfortable, with first and second class options. For those who prefer to travel by bus, companies such as RegioJet and FlixBus offer regular and competitive services.

To get around cities, public transport is an excellent choice. Bratislava, for example, has an efficient network of trams, buses and trolleybuses. A standard ticket allows you to use all public transportation within the city for a limited period, making it easy and convenient to explore the various neighborhoods. For those who want a more flexible option, you can rent electric bikes or scooters, which are available at several stations around the city. The taxi service is also well developed, but it is advisable to use ride-sharing apps such as Bolt or Uber to avoid surprises on costs.

When it comes to accommodation, Slovakia offers a wide range of options to suit all budgets. From the elegant hotel facilities in Bratislava to the cozy guesthouses in the small villages, there is something for every traveler. International chains can be found in larger cities, but for a more authentic experience, consider staying in a guesthouse or bed and breakfast. Many of these places also offer the chance to savor the local cuisine, an option not to be missed. Additionally, platforms such as Airbnb offer a wide selection of apartments for rent, ideal for those looking for more independence during their stay.

Slovak cuisine is a fundamental aspect of the country's cultural heritage and deserves to be explored during your stay. Traditional dishes are often prepared with fresh, local ingredients, providing an authentic experience. Don't miss the opportunity to savor "pierogi", dumplings stuffed with potatoes, cheese or meat, and "kapustnica", a sauerkraut soup typical of the holidays. Local markets and taverns are great places to savor Slovak gastronomy, where you can also buy handicrafts and souvenirs. Slovakia is also famous for its wine production, particularly in the Tokaj region, and for beer, with numerous microbreweries offering tastings.

When it comes to payments, the official currency is the euro, so you won't have to worry about exchanging currency if you're coming from a Eurozone country. Credit cards are widely accepted, but it is advisable to carry cash with you at all times, especially in small shops or markets. ATMs are common and easily available in cities and towns. If you need medical assistance during your stay, the Slovak healthcare system is well organized and the hospital facilities are generally of a good standard. It is advisable to have travel health insurance that covers any unexpected medical expenses.

Slovakia is a safe country for travelers, with a low crime rate. However, as with any other destination, it is important to exercise basic precautions. Avoid leaving valuables unattended and watch out for pickpockets, particularly in crowded areas and public transportation. The local authorities are generally very helpful and ready to assist tourists in case of need. It is always useful to have emergency numbers available, with the general number for emergencies being 112.

The official language is Slovak, a Slavic language, and although many Slovaks speak English, especially in tourist areas and among the younger generation, knowing a few words of Slovak can be very useful and appreciated by the local population. Simple phrases like "Dobrý deň" (Good morning) or "Ďakujem" (Thank you) can help create a bond with the locals and enrich your experience.

Slovakia enjoys a continental climate, with hot summers and cold winters. Summer temperatures can reach 30 degrees Celsius, while in winter they can drop below freezing, especially in mountainous regions. It is advisable to plan your trip according to the activities you plan to do. The summer season is perfect for hiking and outdoor activities, while winter offers opportunities for skiing and winter sports in beautiful mountain resorts such as Jasná and Tatranská Lomnica.

During your stay, also take the time to immerse yourself in Slovak culture. The country is rich in folk traditions, festivals, and cultural events that take place throughout the year. Spring and summer are particularly lively, with numerous music, dance, and craft festivals celebrating the country's rich cultural heritage. Don't miss the chance to visit historic castles, such as Bratislava Castle and Trenčín Castle, which offer not only breathtaking panoramic views, but also a glimpse into Slovak history.

Finally, it is important to respect local customs and cultural norms. Slovaks are known for their hospitality, but it is always good to show respect for traditions and social norms. When visiting a church or place of worship, it is advisable to dress appropriately and follow local directions. During meals, it is customary to wait for the host to start eating before serving.

In summary, Slovakia is a destination that offers a unique mix of natural beauty, history, and culture. With the right practical information, you can explore this fascinating country with ease and enjoy every moment of your adventure. Whether you're exploring the vibrant streets of Bratislava, discovering the stunning landscapes of the Tatra Mountains, or immersing yourself in the traditional village culture, Slovakia promises an unforgettable experience.

Chapter 30: Laws and Local Etiquette in Slovakia

Slovakia, a country rich in history and traditions, offers visitors not only stunning scenery and vibrant culture, but also a set of laws and customs that are important to know for a peaceful and respectful stay. In this chapter, we will explore the main local regulations and customs that characterize daily life in Slovakia, providing a useful framework for those looking to immerse themselves in the reality of the country.

Let's start with the fundamental laws. Slovakia, being part of the European Union, follows many of the common regulations that govern the lives of citizens and visitors. It is essential to have a basic understanding of local laws, especially those related to health, safety, and public behavior. For example, the use of alcohol is allowed, but there are strict restrictions regarding drunk driving. The legal blood alcohol limit for drivers is 0.0%, and penalties for violating this regulation can include hefty fines and license suspension.

Another important law concerns compliance with the rules of conduct in public places. Slovaks value friendliness and good manners, so it is advisable to greet with a smile and a "Dobrý deň" (Good morning) when interacting with the locals. Courtesy is a core value in Slovak culture, and showing respect for locals helps create a friendly atmosphere.

In Slovakia, there are specific laws regarding smoking. Smoking is prohibited in enclosed public places, such as restaurants, bars, and public transportation. However, many venues offer designated smoking areas outside. Visitors should be aware of these restrictions and comply with them to avoid penalties. The Environmental Protection Act is very much felt, and Slovaks are proud of their nature. Therefore, it is essential not to abandon waste and respect public places.

An important topic to consider is photography in public and private places. In Slovakia, it is generally acceptable to photograph landscapes and monuments, but it is advisable to ask permission before photographing people, especially in private settings or during cultural events. Slovaks can be reserved about their privacy, so a courtesy gesture such as asking permission is not only appropriate, but also demonstrates respect for their customs.

Speaking of customs, it is crucial to mention the importance of family and social relationships in Slovak culture. Slovak families tend to be very close-knit, and social gatherings often revolve around shared meals. If you are invited to the home of a Slovak, it is customary to bring a small gift, such as a cake or wine. This gesture is appreciated and shows gratitude for the invitation.

Slovakia is also known for its folkloric traditions, and during local festivals or events, it is common to see traditional dances and costumes. Participating in these celebrations is a great opportunity to immerse yourself in Slovak culture, but it is important to respect customs and follow local directions. For example, during religious events or ceremonies, it is advisable to maintain a dignified and respectful behavior.

An aspect that should not be underestimated is the attitude towards foreigners. Slovaks are generally warm and hospitable, but it is always best to approach them with respect and humility. Conversations about sensitive topics, such as the country's recent history or political issues, should be approached with caution. It is advisable to avoid provocative comments and to maintain an open and respectful attitude towards different opinions.

The official language in Slovakia is Slovak, and although many people speak English, especially in tourist areas, it is always welcome to make an effort to use a few words in Slovak. Simple phrases like "Ďakujem" (Thank you) and "Prosím" (Please) can make a big difference in everyday interactions and demonstrate respect for the local culture.

Slovakia is also a country where public transport is well developed. However, it is important to follow the rules and regulations regarding the use of public transportation. For example, it is mandatory to validate your ticket before boarding, and the penalties for traveling without a ticket can be severe. When traveling, it is a good idea to give up your seat to the elderly or people with disabilities, a gesture that reflects respect for the community.

When it comes to shopping, visitors should be aware of local customs. In commercial establishments, it is common to greet the staff at the entrance and thank them at the time of payment. In local markets, it is customary to bargain, but always with a smile and a certain lightness, so as not to be offensive. Slovak culture values honesty and transparency, so it is advisable to maintain a direct and genuine attitude.

Another myth to dispel concerns the attitude towards money. Slovaks tend to be reserved about their finances, and direct questions about wages or the cost of goods and services may be considered inappropriate. It's best to keep conversations lighter and focus on neutral topics, such as food, travel, or culture.

Finally, it is important to respect the environment and Slovakia's natural traditions. The country is famous for its beautiful national parks and protected areas, such as the Tatra National Park. When visiting these areas, it is crucial to follow the rules regarding hiking and wildlife protection. Leaving no traces, following designated trails, and not disturbing animals are essential behaviors to preserve the country's natural beauty.

In summary, visiting Slovakia offers the opportunity to discover not only a wonderful place, but also a way of life deeply rooted in traditions and mutual respect. Knowing and respecting local laws and customs not only enriches the travel experience, but also helps to create an authentic connection with the Slovak people and their culture. Respecting differences and embracing diversity is what makes every trip unique and memorable.

Chapter 31: Security and Crime Overview in Slovakia

Slovakia, a jewel in the heart of Central Europe, is a nation that offers not only stunning scenery and a rich cultural history, but also a relatively safe environment for travelers. While immersing yourself in the beauty of its castles, mountains, and historic towns, it is crucial to have a clear idea of the security and crime situation in the country. This chapter aims to provide an in-depth and up-to-date analysis of safety in Slovakia, highlighting the positive aspects and any precautions to be taken.

In general, Slovakia is considered one of the safest countries in Europe. Crime rates are relatively low compared to other European nations, making the country an ideal destination for families, couples, and solo travelers. Major cities, such as Bratislava, Košice and Prešov, are generally safe, but, as in any place, it is always advisable to maintain a prudent and conscious behavior.

Crime in Slovakia is mostly minor in nature, with theft and pickpocketing being the most common categories of crime. These accidents mostly occur in crowded areas, such as markets, train stations, and tourist attractions. Therefore, it is important to pay attention to your belongings and not to leave valuables unattended. Vigilance is especially crucial in crowded areas, where opportunistic thieves can take advantage of the distraction of tourists.

Another aspect to consider is the phenomenon of organized crime, which, although present, has a limited impact on the daily lives of citizens and visitors. The Slovak authorities have made considerable efforts to combat this type of crime by improving cooperation between law enforcement agencies and international agencies. The presence of police forces visible on the streets and in tourist areas helps to create an atmosphere of safety and tranquility.

Bratislava, the capital, is one of the most vibrant and dynamic cities in Slovakia. Here, tourists can enjoy a variety of cultural and entertainment events, but it is advisable to remain vigilant, especially during the night. Central areas and entertainment areas can be prone to drunkenness and disorderly behavior, so it is advisable to avoid potentially dangerous situations and move in groups whenever possible. Well-lit streets and efficient public transportation make it easier and safer to get around the city during the evening hours.

The Slovak authorities are very responsive in case of emergencies, and the national emergency number is 112, accessible for any type of critical situation. It's always wise to have a copy of your ID and your health insurance number with you, in case you need medical intervention or law enforcement assistance. Hospitals and clinics in Slovakia are generally of a good standard, and the medical staff is well-trained and helpful.

For travelers looking to explore more rural or mountainous areas, Slovakia offers spectacular natural landscapes, but it's important to be aware of your abilities and prepare properly. Hiking in the mountains, for example, can involve risks, especially in adverse weather conditions. It is advisable to inquire about the conditions of the route and, if necessary, contact the local guides. Using proper equipment and planning ahead can mean the difference between a memorable experience and a dangerous situation.

Slovakia also has a history of ethnic and social tensions, especially in regions with a significant Roma population. While most travelers will never have a problem with this, it's good to be aware of local dynamics and respect different cultures and traditions. Tolerance and mutual respect are core values that can contribute to a positive travel experience.

When it comes to road safety, Slovakia has a good system of roads and highways, but it is important to pay attention to traffic rules. Driving in Slovakia is generally safe, but as in any other country, you may encounter inexperienced or reckless drivers. It is essential to always wear a seat belt and obey speed limits. Weather conditions can affect road safety, especially during the winter, when roads can be icy or snowy. Motorists should ensure that their vehicle is equipped with winter tires during the colder months.

Another aspect to consider is the drug problem, which, although not particularly widespread, can be a concern in some areas. It is not recommended to accept offers of illicit substances and, in the event that they are proposed, it is better to walk away. Slovak law is strict regarding the use and possession of drugs, and the legal consequences can be severe.

In terms of personal safety, it is always advisable to keep a low profile and not flaunt valuables. Using secure bags and keeping important documents in a safe place can reduce the risk of theft. It's also helpful to inquire about areas to avoid, especially at night, and ask residents or hotel staff for recommendations.

Another aspect that should not be underestimated is the importance of communication. Knowing a few basic phrases in Slovak can prove useful, not only to facilitate interactions but also to show respect for the local culture. Although many people speak English, especially in tourist areas, a gesture of courtesy can help create a friendlier and more welcoming atmosphere.

Finally, it's crucial to stay up-to-date on local news and any travel warnings issued by your government. Situations can change quickly, and having timely information can make all the difference in emergencies. Monitoring the news and following the advice of local authorities are always wise practices to ensure a safe and enjoyable trip.

In summary, Slovakia is a fascinating destination that offers a unique travel experience, with a generally safe environment. Being aware of your condition and taking standard precautions can help ensure a peaceful and memorable stay in this country rich in culture and natural beauty. With the right preparation and a cautious attitude, visitors can fully enjoy the wonders that Slovakia has to offer, immersing themselves in its history and people, without having to worry excessively about personal safety.

Don't miss out!

Visit the website below and you can sign up to receive emails whenever Bruna S. T. Smith publishes a new book. There's no charge and no obligation.

https://books2read.com/r/B-A-OQJOC-DANCF

BOOKS 2 READ

Connecting independent readers to independent writers.